Welcome to *Be Your Best*

One of the greatest burdens of my heart is to see God's people enjoy the life Jesus died to give them. I don't want to just hear them talk about it—I want to see them walking in it. I believe it's God's will, based upon Jesus' words, "I came that they may have and enjoy life, and have it in abundance (to the full, till it overflows)" (John 10:10).

Jesus came to give us life as God knows it—full, rich, meaningful, and satisfying. He wants us to be our very best in life—to fully be the person He created us to be. He didn't suffer the scourging, the beatings, and the agony of hanging on the cross so we could live mad, worried, depressed, stressed, frustrated, and aggravated all the time. He died that we might have life and be filled with His joy (see John 17:13).

When I say it's God's will we enjoy our lives, I'm referring to our everyday lives—going to work, driving in traffic,

cooking, cleaning, changing diapers, paying the bills, and teaching our kids to mind. And it's in our ordinary, everyday lives He wants us to be our best. Yes, life has difficulties and disappointments, but God has given us the power of the Holy Spirit, Who lives inside us, to help us live ordinary life in an extraordinary, supernatural way.

To be your best in life involves living your entire life based upon God's value system. It puts your entire being (body, mind, will, emotions, and spirit) right at the top of God's list of important and valuable things. Your entire being plays an important part in God's plan; He's entrusted you to take care of it. Only by keeping our spirits, souls, and bodies in tip-top condition can we truly do God's work.

God wants you to experience the joy of living a balanced life—whether it regards your health, your personal growth, your spirituality, your career and success, your finances, your relationships, or your marriage and family. As you read through these articles, be open to the voice of the Holy Spirit as He points out areas of your life that need to be changed. It may not be easy to change your thinking, but don't give up. God is on your side. By His grace you can become all you were meant to be.

Believing His best for you,

Joyce

Health

Personal Growth

26

100

22

14

Spiritual Maturity

Priorities

117

Finances & Success

Take control of your time and learn to savor the flavor of your life.

Simple steps to small successes lead to big victories.

When it comes to the future, if you and I fail to plan, we plan to fail.

Relationships

How we interact and connect with people to a great degree determines the quality of our lives.

One of the greatest expressions of love you and I can give is forgiveness.

Walking in love is not a feeling or an option or a suggestion—it's a commandment.

Marriage & Family

Uncomplicate your lifestyle, especially in your home, and find power and peace.

Get the advice you need for a lifetime of happiness in your marriage.

Feeling overwhelmed by the responsibilities? God has the answers for all of your parenting challenges.

44

13

78

Balanced Living

Don't let worry pull tomorrow's cloud over today's sunshine.

You can make a decision to be joyful right where you are, with what you have, that transcends your circumstances.

Special Feature

An excerpt from Joyce Meyer's first novel,

"Do something that people don't expect. Don't get in a rut. Keep life fresh and exciting and try doing something outrageously creative..."
— "Ten Steps to Independence"
PAGE 26

All Scripture quotations, unless otherwise indicated, are taken from the Amplified® Bible,
Copyright © 1954, 1958, 1962, 1964, 1965, 1987 by The Lockman Foundation.
Used by permission. (www.Lockman.org)

Scriptures noted NIV are taken from the Holy Bible, New International Version®. NIV®.
Copyright © 1973, 1978, 1984 by International Bible Society.
Used by permission of Zondervan Publishing House. All rights reserved.

Scriptures noted NKJV are taken from the New King James Version.
Copyright ©1979, 1980, 1982 by Thomas Nelson, Inc., Publishers.

Scriptures noted TLB are taken from The Living Bible, copyright © 1971.
Used by permission of Tyndale House Publishers, Inc., Wheaton, Illinois 60189. All rights reserved.

Scriptures noted NLT are taken from the Holy Bible, New Living Translation, 2nd Edition, copyright © 2006.
Used by permission of Tyndale House Publishers, Inc., Wheaton, Illinois 60189. All rights reserved.

Scriptures noted THE MESSAGE are from The Message. Copyright © 1993, 1994, 1995,
1996, 2000, 2001, 2002. Used by permission of NavPress Publishing Group.

Scriptures noted KJV are taken from the King James Version of the Bible.

FaithWords

Hachette Book Group USA

1271 Avenue of the Americas, New York, NY 10020

Visit our Web site at www.faithwords.com.

The FaithWords name and logo are trademarks of Hachette Book Group USA.

Printed in the United States of America.

ISBN: 0-446-58246-8

ISBN-13: 978-0-446-58246-9

LITERARY DEVELOPMENT AND DESIGN:
Koechel Peterson & Associates, Inc., Minneapolis, Minnesota.

Joyce Meyer's Portrait Photography
Dario Acosta

health

thoughts

" If you went to church and the paint was peeling, the doors broken, and the windows boarded, you'd wonder about the pastor, wouldn't you? The church is his instrument for celebrating the glory of God, yet if he doesn't respect the church enough to keep it in good condition, what does this say about his relationship with God?

The same question applies to our bodies. The body is the home of the spirit where God dwells. To do the work God has for us to do, we need to keep it in shape. If we let our bodies get too shabby or sick, we will not be able to experience the presence of God and His joy and peace any more than we could in a run-down church building. Each time we break down emotionally, mentally, or physically, it has a wearing effect on us. If we do it too often, we may eventually come to a place where we can no longer be restored. "

From Nowhere to Now Here

Do you have any idea how valuable you are? If you suffer from self-doubt and self-hatred, if you abuse your body with bad food or bad habits, even if you simply put yourself at the very bottom of the list of people you do things for, then you do *not* understand your own value. If you did, you wouldn't treat yourself that way.

Maybe you never learned your own importance. That's what happened to me. My poor relationship with my body began with sexual, emotional, and mental abuse throughout my childhood. During those years of abuse and fear, I developed a shame-based nature. I felt bad about myself all the time. Those feelings developed into a very dangerous train of thought. Since I didn't like myself or feel attractive, I had no confidence, and I acted like it. I was twenty pounds overweight because I was eating bad food and not exercising, and I didn't feel that I was special enough to make any kind of effort on my own behalf. I looked bad, felt bad, and did nothing to help myself.

At the age of eighteen, I married, left home, and moved more than fifteen times during a five-year period.

My first marriage was extremely stressful. We separated numerous times. He was a heavy drinker, had trouble keeping a job, had affairs with other women, and was a petty thief. I had a miscarriage before later giving birth to a son. When I left the hospital with my baby, I had nowhere to go, so I lived with a relative for a few months. After filing for divorce, I moved back to my parents' house in desperation. I did not realize that all the stress was taking its toll on my body.

> Ask 21st-century women, "How do you feel about yourself?" and many will confess, "I hate myself."

I met Dave Meyer when my son was nine months old, and we were married after a whirlwind courtship of five dates. Obviously, because of all the internal problems I had, the first several years of our marriage were not peaceful. Had Dave not been a committed Christian, I doubt he would have stayed with me.

Though my relationship with God then was not what I now call healthy, I worked hard at it—as I did at everything. I wanted to help people, and God called me into the ministry in 1976 when I was thirty-three years old. As a woman trying to start a new ministry, I experienced opposition from family, friends, and my church. More stress! I threw myself into my ministry full-tilt and worked around the clock, fueling myself with coffee to overcome the sleepiness. It was my way of feeling valuable.

By the time I was thirty-six, I started showing more serious symptoms in my body. I was sick for four months straight. I felt so bad most of the time I could hardly get off the couch. Later I started having hormone imbalances and needed to take shots of estrogen every ten days just to function. Eventually I had a hysterectomy, which immediately plunged me into the change of life.

In 1989 I was diagnosed with breast cancer. The tumor was fast-growing and estrogen-dependent, which meant that not only did I need immediate surgery but also that I could no longer take hormone-replacement therapy while going through early menopause. I had surgery and endured several more years of sheer misery because my hormonal system was such a mess. (Add to that the onset of regular and excruciating migraine headaches—it was like a knife was sticking in my right eye.)

Despite all this I traveled, taught God's Word, stood in faith for my healing, and often wondered how I could go on much longer. I did my duty and worked hard, but I did not enjoy *anything*.

Undoubtedly, part of my problem came from years of fad dieting. Like most people who diet all their lives, I probably lost and gained back a thousand pounds. No one ever taught me the simple truth that "you are what you eat." I was breaking God's laws of health and rest, and He had not given me a special pass that excused me from reaping what I was sowing.

Eventually I started reading books on nutrition. I learned how important food choices are and how dangerous vitamin deficiencies can be, and I became educated on protein, fat, and carbohydrates. Different foods impact your performance, your health, your feelings,

Take the following True/False Quiz to see how your experience and attitudes stack up with that of other women.

TRUE OR FALSE?

1 Most American women get adequate sleep every night.

2 Weekends are the only time women get a break from household responsibilities and chores.

3 Most remarriages don't involve children.

4 Most moms say they spend more quality time with their kids than their own mothers spent with them when they were children.

5 The #1 thing women wish they had more time for is exercise.

6 Most married women are satisfied with the amount of time they spend with their husbands.

7 Time for sex is the #1 thing women miss about married life before kids.

8 Most moms say their husbands are the kind of dads they thought they'd be.

9 Most moms say they—not their husbands—are the problem solvers in their families.

10 The vast majority of moms say they don't have enough time for themselves.

FOR THE ANSWERS, SEE PAGE 11

your looks, and the very makeup of your body. I realized that eating right had to be a way of life, not just a diet I went on to lose some weight, only to return to bad habits and gain it back. I was tired of that cycle. Many of you are tired as well.

Plenty of doctors told me I desperately needed to make some lifestyle changes. But I felt trapped. My ministry work was all-consuming; nothing could be dropped or delegated.

I took nutritional supplements, and I believe they helped me survive—more than any medicines I was given! But since my body was so depleted of health, the only thing the supplements and energy drinks did was shore me up for another day. Stress just kept sucking out everything I put in.

I finally came to the point I was so depleted that if anything stressful happened I would experience shortness of breath and break into a sweat. I cried easily. When my blood pressure hit a dangerous peak, I knew it was time to make some changes.

I cut things from my schedule that weren't bearing fruit. This sounds easy, but it was very hard. After all, I was in charge of an international ministry and felt I needed to be involved in everything that happened. When I finally combined nutritional help with positive lifestyle changes like massage and a more relaxed schedule, I started seeing good results. I got rid of the headaches and neck and back pain. I also experienced an increase in my energy level. But this didn't happen overnight! I had abused my body my entire life, so my health only improved gradually; but just receiving a taste of being better is a powerful motivator.

I wrote my book *Look Great, Feel Great* because I can truthfully say I feel better right now than I ever have in my life! That's a big claim. I live every day passionately, and what a breathtaking change that is. Too many of us get trapped in a rut of negative thinking, believing our healthiest days are behind us. I'm living proof that's not so!

No matter how bad your condition, now is the time to begin to see your physical restoration. There is help! Your body has the ability to restore itself. God will work in you to bring you back to wholeness if you follow His guidelines for good health.

ANSWERS

1 False. Only 15% of women get at least eight hours of sleep a night.

2 False. Half of today's women spend their weekends doing chores and attending to other household responsibilities.

3 False. 65% of remarriages involve children from previous marriages.

4 True. 70% of moms say they spend more time with their kids than their own moms did.

5 False. 69% of moms wish they had more time to enjoy fun activities with their kids. Exercise was a close second—at 67%.

6 False. 79% of women want more time with their husbands.

7 False. Today's moms miss time in bed with their husbands, but many more of them miss sleeping in (69%) than sex (22%).

8 True. 56% of moms say their husbands are the dads they envisioned—although they confess that's not always a positive thing. On the other hand, some of the 44% who gave the opposite answer note their husbands have exceeded their dad-ly expectations.

9 True. This answer might shock some men, but 60% of moms say they are the family problem solvers.

10 True. An overwhelming 90% of today's moms yearn for more self-time.

Answer #3 is taken from *Newsweek*, Jan. 9, 2006, page 47.
The rest of the answers are taken from *Parenting*, Feb. 2006.

thoughts

"Exercise is truly a magic bullet to losing weight, looking our best, and improving our health. I love walking two or three miles in good weather. Not only does that give me the cardiovascular workout essential for long life, it also is a great time to pray, helps me feel more energetic later, and does wonders for my stress level.

Jesus routinely walked from His home in Galilee to Jerusalem—a distance of about 120 miles! Over the course of His ministry, He must have walked thousands of miles. In Jesus' day, people thought little of walking ten miles. And because they did it all their lives, they had the well-developed bodies to accomplish such long walks with ease. "

> "Moderation is the right path in all things."

1. **Make Food Sacred**
   Learn to do everything you do for God's glory, including eating. Look at your plate and ask if what you are about to eat is mostly what God created for you. Make good choices!

2. **Avoid Refined Carbohydrates**
   Obesity, heart disease, and strokes are caused mainly by the huge amount of refined carbohydrates we eat—white flour, potato chips, french fries, and sugar, corn syrup, and other sweeteners. If you simply make an effort to avoid these products, you will do wonders for your health.

3. **Be Fierce About Fruits and Vegetables**
   Make sure you have at least one fruit or vegetable with every meal. Make fruit your snack of choice. For hors d'oeuvres, serve raw vegetables (broccoli, carrots, tomatoes, peppers) with a healthy dip.

4. **Replace Bad Fats with Good Fats**
   The easiest way to make your risk of heart disease plunge is to eat less red meat, dairy, and processed foods made with hydrogenated oils, and eat more fish (twice a week), poultry (turkey breast), olive oil (on bread and in dressings), nuts, and avocados.

5. **Balance Your Plate**
   You can still eat the foods you love; you just need to change the ratio. Salads or vegetables should take up half your plate, while the meat and starch get a quarter each.

5 Ways to Bring Balance to Your Eating

Investing in your health involves investing a little time in learning about healthy foods to eat. It is so important—yet so easy—to eat a healthy, balanced diet. As in all areas of life, common sense is key. One cookie will not bring your health crashing down, but eating full desserts twice every day will have its consequences. Eating healthily simply involves rotating a variety of good foods through your week.

{Mastering Metabolism}
A Guide to Healthy Living and Eating

The Secret to Stable Weight

Have you ever wished you could own a masterpiece, like an original Van Gogh or Monet painting? You may think you could never afford such a masterpiece, but the truth is you were born with one. The human body is God's own masterwork. Part of what makes it so special is its amazing versatility. You were made to survive in all kinds of situations, which is why your body is so adaptable. If you soak up a lot of sun, your body automatically creates extra pigment in your skin to protect you. If you use your muscles every day, your body makes those muscles bigger to help you out. What a system! One way in which your body constantly adapts is through metabolism.

Metabolism is simply the process by which your body breaks down, or metabolizes, your food and converts it into energy. All our energy comes from the food we eat. If you aren't using much energy but are still "filling up your tank" with as much food as usual, you are in trouble. Millions of special, flexible cells throughout your body swell up with the extra fuel, saving it for later. Those are called fat cells. Fat is an extremely efficient way of storing energy for later. Your body can convert any kind of food into fat, store the fat, and then convert the fat back into energy and use it when needed.

The body has another survival trick up its sleeve. Not only does it store energy for lean times in the future, it also tries to be careful about the rate at which it uses these resources. It says, "Whoa, let's slooooooooow things down a little until some good food comes along." It slows your metabolism. And you know what that feels like. You don't want to move. Your brain is groggy. You're cold all the time. You don't do much of anything. You just feel down. And you are burning very few calories, which is great if you are stranded on a desert island, but terrible if you are trying to lose weight.

Why Diets Backfire

You can see why diets wreck metabolism. Any diet that tries to achieve weight loss by drastically cutting back on the number of calories consumed is doomed, because it's based on a misunderstanding of how the human body works. It seems logical enough: eat less, burn more, lose weight. And yes, that is the path to weight loss. The only way to lose weight is to burn more calories per day than we consume. When that happens, the body liquidates your fat reserves and burns them to make up the extra calories. However, not long after you start dieting, your body is going to lower your metabolism to match the new amount of food coming in. This explains the classic dieting dilemma most of us are all too familiar with. You go on a diet and have great success the first few weeks. The pounds fall off and you think you've got it made. But then, even though you are sticking to the diet, suddenly the weight loss

stops. For all these reasons, dieting is not the way to get to, or maintain, a healthy weight.

Five Ways to Boost Metabolism

Exercise. The most effective way to burn more calories is to move. The more regularly you exercise, the higher you keep your metabolism, and the more effortlessly those pounds will melt away. A fringe benefit is you stay alert and happy more of the time.

Eat Breakfast (and lunch and dinner). Breakfast is the most important meal of the day. Think about it: you've fasted for nearly twelve hours. Your metabolism naturally slows down overnight, so breakfast is your body's signal to kick-start itself. A good breakfast gets the machinery working again. All the machinery: digestion, brain power, senses, muscle power. Because a good breakfast makes you so much more active, it can actually help you lose weight. Skipping breakfast just puts you in a state of lethargy. Make sure you get some protein at breakfast; try combining that with a little fat (which keeps you full longer) and fruits or vegetables for vitamins and fiber.

Try changing the equation—eat a substantial breakfast and make dinner the lightest of the three meals—and see if that changes some other numbers, like your weight and waist measurement.

Drink Water. We are all about two-thirds water, and we use water to do everything: to get nutrients to our cells, to cool ourselves off, to flush waste, and to circulate immune cells through the body. Without enough water, all these systems start to suffer, including metabolism. As you begin to dehydrate, you get sluggish, because the water isn't there to transfer fuel to your muscles and brain. If you want to keep your metabolism at a high level, it's essential to get enough water each day.

Sleep Well. Some people believe burning the candle at both ends will help keep them thin, because they burn more calories during the extra awake time. Nothing is further from the truth! People tend to eat more when sleep-deprived because they feel colder and less energetic and mistake these feelings for hunger. Get a decent night's rest and you'll burn more calories overall—and feel a lot better about life.

Fidget. Yes, fidget. Cutting-edge research at the Mayo Clinic has found one of the major differences between overweight people and slender people may be how much they fidget. In other words, it isn't just the planned exercise, such as walks or golf, that make the weight difference, but the hundreds of tiny movements we make—or don't make—during the day. The skinny people tended to "fidget away" 350 calories a day more than the overweight people. That adds up to thirty-five pounds a year!

"If you want to keep your **metabolism** at a high level, it's essential to get enough **water** each day."

{noteworthy}

Sound Advice for a Healthy Lifestyle

Success Strategies

Use your feet. **Think of ways you can get in a little extra walking. Don't ever drive when you can walk. Park so you have to walk a little. Every time you skip the elevator and walk up a flight of stairs, you burn calories, tone some muscles, and wake yourself up too.**

Don't procrastinate. **When you think of a job that needs doing, get up and do it.**

Move more. **Choose activities that force you to move. Try gardening, sweeping the driveway, dance classes, or mall walking. Try putting your TV in front of a treadmill and slowly walk while you watch.**

Stretch. **When you do watch TV, get up and stretch periodically. Do the same thing at work.**

Build Routine. **Keep two five-pound exercise balls close by. Several times a day stop and do a short routine to exercise your upper body.**

Sleep Soundly

Breathe deeply. **Close your eyes, rest your head, and ask God to refresh you. Take a few deep breaths and let your mind calm down.**

Time it right. **Exercise during the day, but not too close to bedtime.**

Set the mood. **Have a quiet household with calming light in the evening.**

Get sleepy. **Don't drink caffeine at night.**

{steps to action: James 1:22}

Be doers of the Word, and not hearers only.

Choose at least one action you can take to boost your metabolism.
Write it down, commit to it, and begin today.

Date	Action	Duration	Comments

" Have you come to an unhappy place in your life? Today can be a new start. God's mercies are new every morning (Lamentations 3:22–23). You can start over at this very moment and live today for the Lord. Determine to follow wherever God leads you, and do whatever He tells you to do. You can expect better tomorrows when you live right today. "

personal growth

CONFIDENCE

Confidence is a wonderful thing.

It allows you and me to face life with boldness, openness, and honesty.

Christians with confidence believe they are loved, valuable, and safe in God's will for their lives. When we feel safe and secure, it's easy to step out and try new things, even though we may make mistakes along the way. Confidence enables us to move forward expecting success rather than fearing failure. It is an essential quality to have in order to fulfill the plans God has for our lives.

One of the main things that hinders us from walking in confidence is self-doubt. Living with self-doubt is like putting your coat on, having someone tie your wrists together, and then trying to take it off. It can't be done. In the same way, the inability to believe in ourselves ties us up in knots and makes it impossible to succeed.

Self-Doubt Is Rooted in Fear

Self-doubt is a tormenting type of fear. It causes us to be afraid of making mistakes or doing the wrong things. For many people, it stems from the fact that they feel wrong about who they are. This deep-rooted feeling can often keep us from accepting ourselves and having the confidence we need to make decisions. As a result, we end up living in confusion and indecisiveness for fear of being wrong.

A person dealing with self-doubt is what God's Word refers to as double-minded. The Bible addresses doubt and double-mindedness in James 1:5–8. It says God cannot answer the prayers of a double-minded man because he is unstable in all his ways. Self-doubt can cause us to shrink back and hide in fear instead of boldly moving forward into what God has for us.

While the enemy uses fear to try and prevent our progress and steal our destinies, God operates through faith to fulfill His call on our lives. Second Timothy 1:7 says, "For God did not give us a spirit of timidity (of cowardice, of craven and cringing and fawning fear), but [He has given us a spirit] of power and of love and of calm *and* well-balanced mind *and* discipline *and* self-control." The first step to walking in confidence is to make up our minds that we will not allow fear to rule our lives. When we determine to walk in God's Spirit—of power, love, and a sound mind—we will begin to tap in to the unshakable confidence found only in Him.

Confidence Is Rooted in Faith

I want to make it clear that our confidence must be in Christ alone—not in ourselves, not in other people, and not in the world or its systems. Our confidence must be rooted in an assurance of God's unconditional love for us. Without the confidence that comes from knowing how much God loves us, we will never really be able to enjoy life or our relationship with Him.

Faith expects good things to happen and enables us to deal with our mistakes. It also enables us to feel safe and live without worry or fear. As our understanding of God's love and grace increases, we become more secure in who we are and are able to face life with the assurance that we can handle whatever comes our way. First John 4:18 says, "There is no fear in love [dread does not exist], but full-grown (complete, perfect) love turns fear out of doors *and* expels every trace of terror!" When we choose to keep our eyes on the Lord, His love for us will drive out fear and self-doubt, enabling us to wait with the confidence He has good things planned for our lives.

"Faith expects

good things

to happen."

Drawing on Confidence in Christ

We can only have confidence as we lean on, trust in, and depend upon the strength of Christ who lives in us. Philippians 4:13 says we can do all things *through Christ* who strengthens us. Confidence is the belief we can do anything God asks because of *His* grace and strength.

Years ago I had a serious problem with a lack of confidence as a result of growing up in a very dysfunctional home. I grew up expecting bad things to happen. I decided that if I expected bad things to happen, I wouldn't feel disappointed when they did. When I moved away from home, I was a brokenhearted person full of self-doubt with a very negative attitude.

Although I believed in God and prayed for His help, I had a lot to learn about believing in God's promises and drawing on confidence in Christ. Thankfully, over the years God changed me, healed me, and gave me a life worth living. He set me free from fear, negativity, and self-doubt. Now, I can't say I never battle with fear or self-doubt, but I have learned I can say NO to them just as easily as I can say YES. And so can you.

"The first step

to walking

in confidence

is to make up

our minds

that we will not

allow fear

to rule our lives."

don't let feelings
rule your life anymore.

The Power of Decision

God created each of us with free will. As believers, we can override all the negative things Satan has planned for us by simply exercising our willpower to agree with God and His Word. The truth is, no matter how doubtful we may feel, we can decide to go forward in faith—confident in God and His Word.

Maybe you had negative messages programmed into your thinking when you were a child like I did. I am here to tell you God can change all that. If you want to enjoy God's best for your life, then start by making a solid decision to resist fear and confidently trust in Him. David said, "By [the help of] God I will praise His word; on God I lean, rely, *and* confidently put my trust; I will not fear" (Psalm 56:4). As you consistently choose to lean on God, believing what His Word says about you more than what others say or how you feel, you will spend less time doubting yourself.

Seeing What God Sees

God's Word says you and I are precious, created in our mother's womb by His own hand (Psalm 139:13). We are valuable and have a purpose on this earth. God says that He has called us by name and we are His (see Isaiah 43:1).

Take a minute and look into your heart. What do you see there? Are you filled with self-doubt, or the confidence that comes from knowing and believing God has a deep and unconditional love for you (see 1 John 4:16)? If your answer does not agree with God's Word, I want to encourage you to begin to renew your mind about how God sees you.

Don't let feelings rule your life anymore. Take a step of faith and start believing God today. Choose to agree with *Him* and believe you are valuable. He has a great future planned for you, and it starts today!

A Confident Woman...

...**knows** God loves her unconditionally.

...**refuses** to live in fear.

...is **positive** in her thinking and acting.

...**recovers** from setbacks.

...**avoids** comparisons to other people.

...takes **action** and overcomes.

...does not **live** in "if only" and "what if."

10 steps to {independence}

We should all be seeking a balanced independence. To me, that is being able to trust and depend on God and other people while still establishing my individual identity. The Bible teaches we are not to be conformed to the pattern of this world (see Romans 12:2). Everyone has their own idea of what we should be. In order to establish a balanced independence in our lives, there are several things we must do.

Break Away from Other People's Expectations

Don't let the people around you determine your values or behavior patterns. Do what God expects you to do and don't live under the tyranny of other's expectations.

Learn to Cope with Criticism

No matter what you do in life, you will be criticized by someone. We must know our own hearts and not allow others to judge us. God alone is our judge.

Do Something Outrageous

Do something people don't expect. Don't get in a rut. Keep life fresh and exciting and try doing some outrageously creative and different things for yourself.

Have Your Own Opinion

Know what you believe and why you believe it. Be wise about how freely you give your opinion and resist letting popular opinion become yours just because it's popular.

Refuse to Pretend

Not being true to oneself is one of the biggest "joy thieves" that exists. To establish independence you must not be a pretender. Be yourself!

Say "No!" When You Need To

A confident person can say "no" when they need to. You need to be aggressive in standing against getting out of balance when others make demands of you.

Spend Time with People Who Give You Space

Find friends who give you space to be yourself and to make mistakes, who respect your boundaries and encourage you in your quest to be an individual.

Watch Children

Jesus said we should become like little children if we expect to enter the kingdom of heaven. Never stop enjoying life and walking in God's wonderful plan for you.

Fight Off Stagnation

Don't just put in your time here on earth. Make the world glad you are here. Whatever it takes for you to keep your life interesting, do it "on purpose."

With God, All Things Are Possible

No matter what happens in your life, remember with God all things are possible. Your confidence must be in Him more than it is in anything or anyone else.

Overcoming Approval Addiction

In his book *The Mask Behind the Mask*, Peter Evans says actor Peter Sellers played so many different roles he forgot his own identity. In other words, he played so many parts he forgot who he was.

Many years ago, I felt similar to Sellers. There were times I felt like a vending machine. Everybody who came by me pushed a different button, expecting a different thing. I wore many masks, trying to be accepted by everyone—my husband, my children, my parents, the people I ministered to, etc. Whatever I thought people wanted me to be is what I tried to be. But it became exhausting and very confusing. One day I was so frustrated I cried out to God and said, "I don't know who I am or how I am supposed to act!" I lost sight of my true identity.

Because I desperately wanted to be loved and approved of by everyone, I said yes to everything anyone asked of me. But I never knew whether someone was going to disapprove of me, and just when I thought I had figured out what they wanted, they changed their minds. Eventually, I became sick from the stress of it all. I was addicted to approval and at the point of burnout.

What Is Approval Addiction?

An addiction is something that controls people—it is something they feel they cannot live without, or something they feel driven to do in order to relieve pressure or pain. Someone addicted to drugs, for instance, will do whatever he needs to in order to get another "fix" when he begins to feel uncomfortable. The addictive substance helps relieve their pain momentarily, but then a damaging controlling cycle starts in their life.

Approval addiction is much the same. When people who are addicted to approval feel unsure and shaky about themselves, they look for a "fix"—they seek out someone to comfort them and reassure them that everything is all right and they are acceptable. And when they meet with disapproval, they go against what they know in their hearts they should do in order to gain approval.

"Don't spend your life angry and bitter."

When a person is addicted to something, it is on their mind most of the time. The greater the addiction, the more that thing consumes their thoughts. If you are addicted to approval, you will have an abnormal concern and an excessive number of thoughts about what people think of you.

What Results from Approval Addiction?

Whatever we are addicted to controls us, and as a result our addiction affects and influences many other areas of our lives. Approval addiction affects not only our personal relationships but also our prayer lives, how we spend our time, and ultimately whether or not we fulfill our destinies. It will certainly steal our peace, joy, and contentment.

When we desperately attempt to keep other people's approval, this often results in feeling used up and pulled in every direction. Anger then begins to build up because we know deep down that what is happening is not right. Ironically, we become angry with those who are pressuring us, but in reality *we* are allowing ourselves to be pressured.

To escape this trap of pressure from others and ourselves, we must take control of our lives and begin following the guidance of the Holy Spirit. He will help us establish proper boundaries—when to say yes and when to say no. You and I cannot live without limits. Even Jesus walked away from the demands of the crowds and made time for renewal.

What Causes Approval Addiction?

Insecurity is one of the greatest causes for approval addiction. People who are insecure want and need the approval of others so much they will do just about anything to get it. A sense of security is something everybody needs and wants. Security enables us to enjoy healthy thinking and living, allowing us to feel safe, accepted, and approved of. When we are secure, we approve of ourselves, we have confidence, and we accept and love ourselves in a healthy, balanced way.

"Many people today live a life of desperation —desperate to fit in, desperate to be accepted, and desperate to be approved of by others."

The atmosphere of the home I grew up in was extremely unstable and supercharged with fear, which left me very insecure. My father was not only abusive but also impossible to please. What he approved of one day (which was rare in itself), I would get in trouble for another day. Experiencing this over and over again turned me into an "approval addict." I became desperate to avoid the pain of disapproval from others.

Insecurity left me frustrated and absent of real peace and joy because I had a poor self-image and felt nobody liked me. Nevertheless, I *acted* as though I didn't need anyone and I didn't care how people felt about me. However, deep down inside I really **did** care, and I tried very hard to please them.

What changed my thinking? I began studying the Word of God and learning who I am in Christ. I learned to see myself the way God sees me—as the righteousness of His Son Jesus (see 2 Corinthians 5:21). I meditated on scriptures that showed me how much God loved me and approved of me...even *before* I was born (see Jeremiah 1:5; Romans 5:8). God's truth set me free, and for the first time I began to feel secure in Him.

"Don't fight with addictions, but instead refuse to feed them."

How Can You Have a Healthy Relationship?

Relationships are a very valuable part of our lives, and God desires us to have healthy, enjoyable ones. What you and I allow in our relationships in the beginning should be what we will be happy with permanently. That's wisdom—choosing now what we will be happy with later on. Let people know by your actions that even though you would like their approval, you can live without it if needed. Give others respect, while letting them know that you also expect them to show you respect.

Any relationship where one person is in control while the other struggles to gain approval is unhealthy. We should not "buy" friends by letting them control us. If we do, whatever we did to get them we will have to continue doing. You and I should never sin against our own consciences, doing something we know and feel in our hearts is wrong, in order to have someone's approval. This is not right, and it is not God's will.

There will be times in our relationships when confrontation is needed. In other words, we will have to say no to something even when the other person wants to hear yes. If you have not been confronting, and you now find yourself being controlled and manipulated, making this change will take time. I encourage you to begin praying about it, asking God to give you courage to speak the truth in love and help the other person be willing to accept your decision and change.

Remember, breaking any addiction will cause suffering, but it leads to victory. At first, you may feel very uncomfortable with the thought of someone not being happy with you, but keep in mind that your only other choice is spending your life being unhappy. Don't waste your pain—suffer for what is going to produce something good in your life.

Will You Accept the Challenge?

I challenge you to trust God to bring you friends. Sometimes we want to be in relationship with a person who looks good on the outside, but then the relationship turns out to be a nightmare. So instead of working yourself silly trying to build relationships with the people you think would make good friends, give your relationships to God. He may surprise you by connecting you with people you would have never chosen to be in relationship with but feel closer to you than your own family.

I also encourage you to pray for favor. Psalm 5:12 says the Lord blesses the righteous and surrounds them with a shield of favor. Begin confessing you have favor with both God and man. When God gives us favor, He gives us things we don't deserve in the natural, including quality relationships.

Don't seek to be a people pleaser...don't compromise what you know is right in your heart to gain the approval of others. The only approval you need is the Father's, and that you already have. As you make it your aim to please God, any addiction to approval you have will break under the power of His love...it's only a matter of time.

"Let people know by your actions that even though you would like their approval, you can live without it if needed."

{steps to action: James 1:22}

Be doers of the Word, and not hearers only.

Is there an area of your life where you have an approval addiction?
If so, state it as clearly as you possibly can.

What results do you experience from your approval addiction?

What causes you to feel and act this way?

Search God's Word and write out scriptures that counter the lies
you have been believing.

Declare how you will apply God's truth when you feel the next urge
to be a people pleaser.

[cracked pots]

GOD WORKS THROUGH JARS OF CLAY, or what I often call "cracked pots." This means we are flawed, so when people look at us and see amazing things happening, they know it must be God at work because it certainly could not be us.

"However, we possess this precious treasure [the divine Light of the Gospel] in [frail, human] vessels of earth, that the grandeur *and* exceeding greatness of the power may be shown to be from God and not from ourselves."

—2 CORINTHIANS 4:7

I believe anyone who really knows me doesn't have any difficulty realizing that the work I am doing on the earth today certainly must be God at work in and through me. They give Him the glory, not me, because they see my imperfections and know my limitations. God chooses the weak and foolish things on purpose so no mortal can have pretense for glorying in His presence (see 1 Corinthians 1:27–29).

Imagine a covered pot with a lamp inside it. Even though the pot may be filled with light, no one can see the light within it. Yet if the pot is cracked, the light will shine through the cracks. In this same way, God works through our imperfections.

Can you love a cracked pot? God can. It is godly to love yourself in a balanced, healthy way. It is ungodly to reject and despise yourself.

Seek to be what I call an "everything-nothing" person—everything in Christ and nothing without Him. Jesus said, "Apart from Me...you can do nothing" (John 15:5). Be confident in Christ and remain humble. I know I can do nothing of any real value unless Christ is flowing through me. Always give God the credit for your success.

"When God created Adam and Eve, He blessed them, told them to be fruitful and multiply and use all the vast resources of the earth in the service of God and man. Are you being fruitful? Is your life causing increase? When you get involved with people and things, do they increase and multiply? Some people only take in life, and they never add anything. I refuse to be that kind of person. I want to make people's lives better.

Are you using the resources God has given you? We must all make sure we are not like the rich man in the Bible who had so much all of his barns were full with no room for more. Instead of giving any of it away, he decided to build bigger barns and collect more for himself. I think he was the dumbest man in the Bible."

thoughts

the battle belongs
to the Lord

a four-phase battle plan for walking in daily victory

THERE ARE TIMES IN OUR LIVES when we feel we are up against what seems to be an insurmountable enemy. Things appear to be hopeless, and we are in a fight we think we can't possibly win. It's in times like these that we need to remember, the battle belongs to the Lord.

You and I are involved in a spiritual war in the unseen realm (see Ephesians 6:12). But the Bible also makes it clear that no matter what we may be facing, God has a plan. His plan for us is to be victorious—even when our problems *feel* overwhelming. You may be struggling with fear, a bad habit, poverty, relationship issues, or even a life-threatening disease. Whatever it is, when you give your battle to the Lord, you put yourself in a position for victory.

One of the best examples in Scripture concerning overcoming insurmountable enemies is found in 2 Chronicles 20. Here we find Jehoshaphat, king of Judah, receiving the news that a vast army of Moabites and Ammonites was coming to attack. There are four basic phases to God's battle plan which are instructive for us. Let's look at them.

PHASE 1	**PHASE 2**	**PHASE 3**	**PHASE 4**
Seek a Word from the Lord	Depend on the Lord	Give Glory to the Lord	Expect Deliverance from the Lord

Phase 1
of God's Battle Plan
Seek a Word from the Lord

Facing an overwhelming enemy army, King Jehoshaphat was afraid initially, but he did not allow fear to paralyze him. "Then Jehoshaphat feared, and set himself [determinedly, as his vital need] to seek the Lord; he proclaimed a fast in all Judah" (2 Chronicles 20:3). Jehoshaphat pushed past his fear and determined to seek the Lord for a word. He knew only God could give him a plan sure to succeed.

Notice Jehoshaphat began his prayer in verses six and seven by declaring who God was, acknowledging how great He was, and even reviewing the mighty things He had done for His people. Then Jehoshaphat expressed his confidence in the Lord to handle the problem.

When trouble comes and we know we are facing an attack of the enemy, our first response should be to seek a word from the Lord. We need to resist trying to reason or figure things out in our mind or running to people for the answer. Yes, God may direct us to a person for advice, but we should always go to Him *first* to show that we honor and trust Him. When we hear from God, faith fills our hearts and drives away fear like nothing else.

Phase 2
of God's Battle Plan
Depend on the Lord

The second step of King Jehoshaphat was to admit to God his total inability to deal with the problem. He does this in 2 Chronicles 20:12: "O our God, will You not exercise judgment upon them? For we have no might to stand against this great company that is coming against us. We do not know what to do, but our eyes are upon You."

There are three very important things Jehoshaphat did in this verse. First, he admitted he had no might to stand against his enemies. Second, he admitted he did not know what to do. And third, he said their eyes were on God. These three things put Jehoshaphat and the people of Judah in a position for a miracle. In a similar way, after we set ourselves to seek a word from God, we need to *realize that we are totally dependent on Him* to solve our problem.

One of the spiritual laws of receiving from God is learning to totally depend upon Him. In John 15:5 Jesus said, "Apart from me you can do nothing" (NIV). This is a scripture God showed me early in my walk with Him. I was a very independent person, and it took me a while to realize how totally dependent on God we really are. Sometimes we face situations, like cancer, that we *know* we can do nothing about. Other times we face things we *think* we "can handle." But the truth is, we are dependent upon God for grace to succeed in *every* situation.

I recall a time years ago when I went to the doctor for a regular checkup, and they found a small lump in my breast. When they tested it and discovered it was a fast-growing type of cancer, I was suddenly faced with not only the prospect of surgery but also a battle with overwhelming fear. I can still remember walking down the hall in my house and fear hitting me so hard I felt I was going to fall down. It was so strong I had a hard time sleeping at night. I was desperate—in a fight for my life.

One night, as I was lying awake in my bed at about three o'clock in the morning, God impressed deep inside my heart, "Joyce, you can trust Me." As a result of this one word from the Lord, I was delivered from overwhelming fear. Although I was apprehensive as I waited for test results, I knew I was in God's hands and that whatever happened He would take care of me.

Phase 3
of God's Battle Plan
Give Glory to the Lord

Jehoshaphat's third step in God's battle plan for victory was to get in the right position—the position of praise to God. In 2 Chronicles 20:17 the Lord spoke to Jehoshaphat and said, "You shall not need to fight in this battle; take your positions, stand still, and see the deliverance of the Lord [Who is] with you, O Judah and Jerusalem."

After receiving this instruction from the Lord, Jehoshaphat immediately bowed on his knees with his face to the ground and worshipped God. Like Jehoshaphat, when we are faced with insurmountable enemies, we need to get in position and worship God. In other words, whether we bow on our knees like Jehoshaphat or stand with our hands lifted, our battle position is one of praise and worship. Love, joy, peace, God's Word, prayer—all of these are weapons of warfare.

Often, when the Israelites went to battle, they sent Judah first. The meaning of the name *Judah* is "praise." Sending Judah first symbolizes praise leading the way. In 2 Chronicles 20:21 we read that King Jehoshaphat instructed singers to go out in front of the army praising God and giving Him thanks. Singing and giving thanks may not *feel* like the thing to do when we are in trouble, but it is exactly what we *need* to do.

Phase 4 of God's Battle Plan

Expect Deliverance from the Lord

If you continue to read Jehoshaphat's story in 2 Chronicles 20, you'll see the final phase of God's battle plan is to obey any instructions He gives us and expect deliverance from the Lord. Then we can watch with an attitude of faith for victory from Him. As Jehoshaphat and the people of Judah followed God's battle plan, the Lord delivered them from their enemies. How did they defeat their enemies? When Jehoshaphat appointed singers to sing and praise at the head of Judah's army, the Lord defeated their enemies by confusing them so much they killed each other!

When you are faced with a battle and you don't know what to do, follow the battle plan God gave Jehoshaphat and the people of Judah. First, seek God for a word from Him. Next, acknowledge your dependence upon Him to bring you through to victory. Third, take your position—worshiping God and giving Him thanks. Finally, watch and expect God to move on your behalf (see Isaiah 30:18). As you worship God, you will be in a position to not only win your battles but also enjoy your walk with Him and your everyday life more than ever!

Years ago I was struggling with severe headaches, and the doctor put me on medication. The medicine made me feel sick to my stomach and caused a loud roaring noise in my head. I felt I was going crazy. One night, I felt so sick I went into the bathroom and sat with my head resting on the toilet seat. Just then I heard a song coming up from within, and the Holy Spirit said, "Sing." At that moment, I felt a lot more like throwing up or giving up than singing. But I chose to obey God, and I started feeling better.

It's easy to praise and worship God after being delivered from a problem—when the headache is gone or our enemies are defeated. But worshiping before the battle is actually won really gets God's attention.

spiritual
maturity

We serve an awesome God! He is El Shaddai, the almighty God—the All-Sufficient One Who has absolute power over everything. There is nothing too difficult for Him. He is Jehovah Jireh, the Lord Who Provides. He has made available to use as believers a limitless supply of love, joy, peace, wisdom, grace, finances, and every other spiritual and material blessing. The Bible says in Psalm 23 the Lord is our Shepherd, and He desires to provide for us in such a way our "cup" runs over.

Living the

Although this abundant life is available to all believers, many are not experiencing it. I put my faith in Jesus Christ at age nine and started going to church at twenty-six, but I didn't really begin to experience the abundant life Jesus died to give us until I was in my midforties. What brought about the change? There are a number of reasons, and two of the biggest ones are that I learned the importance of living by faith and walking in obedience.

Live by Faith

Developing an attitude of faith is one of the most important requirements to experiencing abundance or overflow in our lives. An attitude of faith is more than just believing in God for something we need when we need it—it is a *lifestyle* of trusting God for everything. There is a difference. Although you and I may begin our walk with God because we need Him to meet our needs and solve our problems, somewhere along the way we need to begin seeking and serving Him because He is our life. In other words, we come to realize our very existence depends on Him.

Living by faith is what justifies us before God and puts us in right relationship with Him. Romans 1:17 says,

Abundant Life

"I came that they may have and enjoy life,
and have it in abundance
(to the full, till it overflows)."

—JOHN 10:10

"This Good News tells us how God makes us right in his sight. This is accomplished from start to finish by faith. As the Scriptures say, 'It is through faith that a righteous person has life'" (NLT). This means our relationship with God is a lifestyle that leads us from one level of faith to another level of faith.

Stop the Enemy's Interference

Now, it's important to realize that all along the way, Satan tries to interrupt or sidetrack our walk of faith with doubt, fear, confusion, and unbelief. His aim is to get us to stop believing and trusting in God's faithfulness and His promises, and get us to focus on things in the natural, such as our jobs, our finances, our families, our health, and on and on. Why does Satan work so diligently to interrupt our faith? Because by doing so, he interrupts our fellowship with God and cuts off the

flow of God's blessings. If he can get us to stop believing and trusting in God's goodness, then he can successfully steal our peace and joy. Why? Because joy and peace are found in believing (see Romans 15:13).

I lived many years of my early Christian walk going from faith to doubt to unbelief to fear and then back to faith again. There were times when I was believing God to bring change or provision in my life, and Satan would whisper thoughts of doubt, fear, and confusion into my mind. Once I accepted his lies, I'd move from living by faith to living in unbelief. But because God's Spirit lives in me, He didn't leave me alone in unbelief. Sooner or later, He would stir me up and bring me around full circle and put me back on a track of believing. Eventually, I realized that as you and I stay in faith, we have a steady supply of power, peace, and joy, and we put ourselves in position to reap the rewards of the abundant life Jesus died to give us.

Walk in Obedience

Another very important ingredient to experiencing a life that is running over with the blessings of God is obedience—doing what we know in our heart is right. Ephesians 3:20 (NLT) says, "Now all glory to God, who is able, through his mighty power at work within us, to accomplish infinitely more than we might ask or think." Now this is a wonderful promise, but it

Satan works diligently to interrupt our faith because by doing so he interrupts our fellowship with God and cuts off the flow of God's blessings.

is only fulfilled if we cooperate with the power of the Holy Spirit to make the needed changes in our thoughts, words, and actions.

Letting God's power work in us doesn't mean feeling goose bumps in a church service. It means choosing *not* to live by what we want, think, and feel, but by what we know is right in our spirit. Many times this knowing in our spirit is based on specific scriptures; other times it comes from a specific prompting of the Holy Spirit.

Make a Positive Confession

God is no respecter of persons, and He has an awesome life planned for you (see Jeremiah 29:11; Romans 2:11). I encourage you to stop settling for less than God's very best. Make a solid decision to live by faith and walk in obedience to what you know is right. The next time Satan tries to interrupt your faith, open your mouth and say, "No, Satan. I'm not going to receive any of your lies—you're not going to interrupt my faith. God is faithful and true, and He will come through for me again—just as He did countless times before. I'm going to *receive* God's grace, *believe* His Word, and *do what's right.*" With this type of confession, peace, power, and hope will be released, and before long, God's glory—His manifested excellence—will be revealed in your life!

When God says, "Go," get going.

Two decades ago, God prompted me to leave the church in St. Louis where I was the associate pastor and take my ministry north, south, east, and west. Now this was very scary for me because to leave that church meant leaving all I knew and was comfortable with. Almost immediately, my flesh reasoned against it. I thought, *Well, what if nobody comes to my meetings? No one knows me outside of my church. Where are we going to get the money?* With many unanswered questions, doubts, and fears, I decided not to go.

Even though God gave me confirmation after confirmation—through friends and even total strangers—I chose not to leave. Little by little, I began to lose the joy, peace, and anointing I once had. One day, after about a year passed, I cried out to God and asked, "What's wrong with my life? I feel like Your anointing is lifting off me. What's going on?"

"I told you to leave a year ago, and you're still here. I'm finished with you here, and it's time for you to move on" was God's message to me. At that point, I chose to obey God and leave. That act of obedience opened the door to the abundant life I'm now living. Had I not left that church, I don't believe I would be where I am today—ministering to millions of people around the world.

Throughout our lives, we all experience different degrees of mistreatment. Whether it is a minor hurt or major abuse, each fiery offense tends to leave us "burnt" in one way or another. As burned wood leaves behind ashes, hurt leaves us with a pile of emotional and mental ashes we must deal with.

beauty
for ashes

*"To all who mourn...he will give: **Beauty** for ashes; **Joy** instead of mourning; **Praise** instead of heaviness."* —ISAIAH 61:3 TLB

"May you be rooted deep in love and founded securely on love, that you may have the power and be strong to apprehend and grasp with all the saints [God's devoted people, the experience of that love] what is the breadth and length and height and depth [of it]."

—EPHESIANS 3:17-18

I was sexually, physically, verbally, mentally, and emotionally abused by a number of men from my earliest childhood through the age of twenty-three. I have been rejected, abandoned, betrayed, and divorced. The abuse I experienced left behind many ashes. I became controlling, manipulative, angry, critical, negative, overbearing, and judgmental. I was filled with self-pity, bitterness, and depression, and I was verbally abusive.

Abuse leaves a person emotionally handicapped—it renders them unable to maintain healthy, lasting relationships without intervention of some kind. I wanted desperately to receive and give love, but I was unable. Even after I met and married my "knight in shining armor," Dave Meyer, I was still a mess mentally and emotionally. Don't get me wrong. I worked and functioned in society like many others, went to church, and loved Jesus. But I didn't have any peace, joy, or victory in my everyday life.

The sad part is, I thought everybody else had a problem. I did not know that the problem was really within me.

Rotten Fruit Is Produced from Rotten Roots

In order to exchange our ashes for God's beauty, we must first realize the "fruit," or behavior, in our lives comes from our roots. Bad behavior is like bad fruit produced from a bad tree with bad roots. If you are dealing with undesirable behavior, ask yourself what type of things you experienced growing up at home. In school. In past relationships. In church. If they were hurtful or abusive to any degree, God wants to uproot you from the pain of those experiences and transplant you in the good soil of Jesus Christ.

The Word says, "May you be rooted deep in love *and* founded securely on love, that you may have the power *and* be strong to apprehend *and* grasp with all the saints [God's devoted people, the experience of that love] what is the breadth and length and height and depth [of it]" (Ephesians 3:17–18).

I had plenty of "rotten fruit" in my life that was hurting not only me but also those around me. Simply "picking the fruit" did not work. I would try and behave correctly to get rid of the visibly bad behavior, but another one would pop up in another area of my life. In order to truly get rid of the fruit, we have to get rid of the roots, which is painful at times. Being transplanted, rooted, and grounded in Christ is a *process* that *takes time*.

True Healing Comes from Understanding God's Perfect Love

Years ago, when I was reading the Bible one day, the Holy Spirit stopped me and asked me, "What do you believe, Joyce, about your relationship with God? Do you believe He loves you?" This made me take a serious look at what I really believed about God's love for me. I came to the conclusion that although I did believe He loved me, I thought He did so *conditionally*—that my behavior influenced His love for me.

Thankfully, as I studied His Word, I began to see the truth that God's love for us is unconditional. I learned that the mistreatment and abuse from others is *not* a reflection of God's love. His perfect love for us is not based on our perfect behavior or anything else. His

> "God will take every broken piece of our lives and use them for good... if we let Him."

love for you and me is based on Him and Him alone. God *is* love—it is Who He is. Although we often stop receiving God's love when our behavior is bad, God never stops loving us.

First John 4:16 says, "And we know (understand, recognize, are conscious of, by observation and by experience) and believe (adhere to and put faith in and rely on) the love God cherishes for us. God is love, and he who dwells *and* continues in love dwells *and* continues in

God, and God dwells *and* continues in him." This is a key scripture for me because it says we should be conscious and aware of God's love and put faith in it. As I went through life's experiences and meditated on God's Word, I put more and more faith and confidence in His never-ending love for me.

Realize the devil's goal is to separate us from God's love, because God's love is the main ingredient in our emotional healing. But don't let him succeed. You and I were created for God's love and fellowship, and if we will trust His love is always flowing toward us, nothing will be able to separate us from it (see Romans 8:35, 38–39).

God Will Use Every Fragment of Your Broken Life for Good!

Abuse and mistreatment from others can leave our lives broken and shattered in pieces. Our thoughts, our emotions, and

our dreams can all become fragments of what they were meant to be. But thankfully we serve a God Who wastes nothing. After Jesus fed the five thousand, He told His disciples, "Gather up now the fragments (the broken pieces that are left over), so that nothing may be lost *and* wasted" (John 6:12). I believe there is a spiritual principle here we can also apply to our lives. God will take every broken piece of our lives and use them for good…if we let Him.

My life was severely broken and fragmented by fear, insecurity, emotional addictions, and a deep-rooted sense of rejection. Over time, as I yielded myself to God, He took my fragmented life and turned my mess into my message. Now, I have the privilege of teaching His people how to break free from every hang-up and pain of the past and be whole in Him.

As you surrender your life to Him daily, He will bind up your wounds and heal your bruises. His Word is medicine for your soul…it brings healing to your mind, your will, and your emotions. Proverbs 4:20–22 says, "My son, attend to my words; consent *and* submit to my sayings. Let them not depart from your sight; keep them in the center of your heart. For they are life to those who find them, **healing *and* health** to all their flesh." I can't say it enough that true freedom comes from abiding in God's Word—meditating, memorizing, and applying specific scriptures to our specific wounds (see John 8:31–32).

What Are You Doing with Your Ashes?

Whether you were hurt five minutes ago or fifty years ago, you will always need to make a decision about what you are going to do with the residue. Mistreatment and abuse leave behind "ashes" which can often manifest in an endless number of addictive behaviors. What ashes are you dealing with in your life? Are you dealing with an eating disorder or with excessive fear or a tendency to work too much?

In order to exchange your ashes for God's beauty and truly break free from their effects, you must deal with the root causes...you must allow the Holy Spirit to surface the issues from your past where you need healing. The Holy Spirit knows *what* to bring to your memory and *when*. His timing is perfect, and when it is time to deal with something, He will give you the power to deal with it.

If you are ready to begin the healing process or pick up where you left off, Jesus stands ready and willing to heal you. "To all who mourn...he will give: **Beauty** for ashes; **Joy** instead of mourning; **Praise** instead of heaviness" (Isaiah 61:3 TLB). I encourage you to pray a prayer like this:

Lord, I believe You love me and You can take all the broken pieces of my life...the ashes...and make something good out of them. In Romans 8:28 your Word says, "All things work together and are [fitting into a plan] for good to and for those who love God and are called according to [His] design and purpose." I

love You, Lord. Forgive me for the hurts I have caused others. I receive Your forgiveness now. Help me forgive those who have hurt me. Lord, I receive Your healing for my broken heart. In Jesus' name.

My friend, God loves you with an everlasting, unconditional love. He WILL heal you...everywhere you hurt. Surrender your life to Him today and every day. Pour your heart out to Him in prayer. Spend time meditating on, memorizing, and speaking His Word. Believe what *He* says about you in His Word instead of believing how you feel or what others say. As you do, you will be transformed into a triumphant trophy of God's grace!

experience the love of God

God loves you! I want to say it again. God *loves* YOU! Not only does He love you, but He also has a wonderful plan for your life. I want to show you from Scripture what the God of all creation thinks about you. Why is this so important? Because whatever God thinks and says about us is what we should also think and say about us. I believe as you meditate on and memorize these scriptures, your self-image will be changed, and as a result, your present and future will be changed too.

how can I really know God loves me?

Here are some practical suggestions for helping you develop a conscious awareness of God's unconditional love for you:

- **Tell yourself in your mind and out loud, "God loves me."** Say it over and over a few times, and let it sink in—especially when you don't feel like He loves you. Look at yourself in the mirror, point to yourself, and say, "[Your name], God loves you."

- **Pray for the Holy Spirit, Who is our Teacher, to give you a revelation of God's love.** See John 14:26; 16:13.

- **Read some good books about God's love.** Consider starting with one of my books, *Reduce Me to Love.*

- **Keep a diary, a book of remembrance, of the special things God does for you.** Include little things as well as major things. Read over your list at least once a week, and you will be encouraged.

- **Learn and commit to memory several Bible verses about God's love for you.** Here are some to help you get started: Psalm 139:17–18; Isaiah 49:16; Jeremiah 1:5; Romans 5:5, 8; 8:33–35, 38; Ephesians 2:4–6; 3:17–19; 1 John 4:16–18.

God's Eyes Are Constantly on You

In Isaiah 49:16, God says, "Behold, I have indelibly imprinted (tattooed a picture of) you on the palm of each of My hands"; and in Psalm 139:17–18, David says, "How precious are your thoughts about me, O God! They are innumerable! I can't even count them; they outnumber the grains of sand!" (NLT). Just as a proud parent or grandparent carries pictures of their children and/or grandchildren in their wallets, God carries a picture of you on the palms of His hands. Isaiah 30:18 says that "the Lord [earnestly] waits [expecting, looking, and longing] to be gracious to you; and therefore He lifts Himself up, that He may have mercy on you *and* show loving-kindness to you." He is always thinking about you—He's constantly looking for ways to bless and teach you as well as correct and direct you.

God's Love Will Never Fail

No matter what you're going through in life or how difficult the circumstances may be, God's love is constantly flowing toward you. Isaiah 54:10 says, "For though the mountains should depart and the hills be shaken *or* removed, yet My love *and* kindness shall not depart from you, nor shall My covenant of peace *and* completeness be removed, says the Lord, Who has compassion on you." The apostle Paul echoes this promise in Romans 8:38–39: "For I am persuaded beyond doubt (am sure) that neither death nor life, nor angels nor principalities, nor things impending *and* threatening nor things to come, nor powers, nor height nor depth, nor anything else in all creation will be able to separate us from the love of God which is in Christ Jesus our Lord."

God's Love Can Only Be Received, Not Earned

It is a free gift. Once you realize you're loved by God unconditionally, you can quit trying to earn His love or feeling like you deserve His love and simply *receive* it and enjoy it. There is nothing that we can do to make God love us any less or any more than He already does. Start confessing out loud several times a day that God loves you and accepts you. Speaking this truth out into the atmosphere will help you believe it and line up your will with God's will. Proverbs 18:21 says the power of life and death is in the tongue. When you begin to say out loud, "God loves and accepts me," your soul becomes saturated with life. As a result, the way you think and feel about yourself begins to change.

God Has Loved You Since the Beginning of Time

"Even before he made the world, God loved us and chose us in Christ to be holy and without fault in his eyes. [God decided in advance] to adopt us into his own family by bringing us to himself through Jesus Christ. [This is what he wanted to do, and it] gave him great pleasure" (Ephesians 1:4–5). What a joy it is to know God has always

loved us and He chose to adopt us and make us His own even before the world began!

My friend, God loves you greatly and is trying to reveal His love to you right now. Open your heart and receive His love. He accepts you right where you are. He never rejects or condemns those who rely on and trust in Him (see John 3:18). As you confess these scriptures out of your mouth and over your life, you will bring your will into agreement with God's will. This puts you in position to fulfill your destiny and receive all Jesus died to give you.

{steps to action: James 1:22}

Be doers of the Word, and not hearers only.

Do you believe...in your heart and with all your heart that God loves you unconditionally? Write out your thoughts.

How do you feel when you read that God the Father has "indelibly imprinted (tattooed a picture of) you on the palm" of each of His hands (Isaiah 49:16)?

Search God's Word and write out scriptures that describe God's love for you.

Describe how your life will be different as you experience God's love daily.

priorities

DEVELOP
THE POWERFUL
POTENTIAL

{in You}

"All our **dreams** can come true, if we have the **courage** to pursue them."

— WALT DISNEY —

There is a gold mine of potential hidden deep within every person, and you are no exception. When God created you and me, He breathed the breath of life into us and then placed a little part of Himself in us. We are created in His image and filled with His potential—a potential to do the impossible.

But how do we harness it? How can we turn possibilities into realities? First of all, we need to recognize what stands in the space between having potential and seeing it fully develop, and that is time, determination, and hard work.

What Is Potential?

Potential is "greatness that exists as a possibility but is not yet a reality." In other words, a person who has potential has all the necessary ingredients to be successful, but the ingredients have not yet been activated. It's like knowing there is a huge vein of gold hidden in the earth in your yard. But in order to get to it and fully benefit from its tremendous value, you have to do some deep digging. The person with untapped potential needs something to motivate them to take action and bring to the surface the treasure within them.

To a great degree, our God-given potential is directly connected to our dreams and visions. God plants them in our heart, or spirit, as a seed in the form of a thought or desire. Over time, the seed grows as we feed it, but we must be very careful to watch over and protect it from the enemy who is a master at stealing dream seeds.

When God called me into ministry, I didn't know where to start, much less finish. However, as God gave me anointed ideas and opened up doors of opportunity to serve, I stepped out in faith. I learned to stop looking to myself for answers and start looking to God. Each time, He provided me with the strength, wisdom, and ability I needed to be successful.

"It's not what you've got, it's what you use that makes a difference."

— ZIG ZIGLAR

Drawing on God's Strength Is Essential

You and I cannot fully develop our potential without the power of God at work in us. Therefore, we must learn to draw on God's strength every day. Ephesians 6:10 says, "Be strong in the Lord [be empowered through your union with Him]; draw your strength from Him [that strength which His boundless might provides]." From this verse, we are promised that the Holy Spirit will pour strength into our inner man...our human spirit...as we spend time "in union," or fellowshiping, with God.

How do we spend time with God? It starts with a daily choice to be with Him. It includes things like reading and studying Scripture, singing songs of thanks and praise to Him, talking to and listening to Him in prayer, and then leaving an open line of communication with Him throughout the day. Sometimes spending time with God is simply sitting quietly and looking at His creation.

There is nothing on earth that can offer the refreshing rewards of spending time with God. No relationship, no vacation, no amount of money, no job...nothing can even come close to the blessings of strength that come from a relationship with Him.

Working Hard Is Also Important

To achieve our potential, you and I must give it some form. Like wet cement, our potential must be poured into something in order for it to have shape and become useful. To develop our potential properly, we must have a purpose and a plan, and we must be doing something to fulfill it. These things are our "form," and prayer must cover the whole thing. It takes hard work and solid ongoing decisions to bring form to our potential.

Deion Sanders is the only athlete to have hit a Major League home run and scored an NFL touchdown in the same week. Sanders grew up on the tough streets of Fort Myers, Florida, where he was exposed to some "would-be" athletes who spurred him to make a success of himself. He explains: "I call them I'das. 'If I'da done this, I'd be making three million today. If I'da practiced a little harder, I'd be a superstar.' They were as fast as me when we were kids, but instead of working for their dreams, they chose drugs and a life of street corners. We don't need any more I'das."

I believe many people are unhappy because they are not doing anything to develop their potential. Don't let this happen to you. Grab the moments you have—begin doing something with your potential. Remember, your potential is directly connected to your gifts and calling. If you are unsure of what your call is, start doing a few things in the area you are interested in...step out into what you feel God is leading you to do. You will soon discover what you can and cannot do. You can rest assured that God will not call you to spend your whole life doing something you hate or can't do.

Experience the Power of Patience

What does patience have to do with developing your potential? A lot. Without patience, you and I are going to fall short at developing and reaching our fullest potential. Patience is a fruit of God's Spirit which manifests itself in a calm, positive attitude. It is not the ability to wait; it is the ability to keep a good attitude while we wait. And according to Hebrews 10:36, you and I need patience so that we "may perform and fully accomplish the will of God."

Just think of cooking a pot of stew. You could fill the pot with pure filtered water, fresh vegetables, choice seasonings, and the finest cuts of meat available. All the necessary ingredients are in the pot to make an outstanding stew. But only time and the proper temperature will allow the ingredients to cook and blend together to produce the rich-tasting, full-flavored stew desired.

The same is true with you and me. God brings tests and trials into our lives to develop patience in us. During the process, He is blending all our ingredients, or potential, into a rich, full-flavored expression of Who He is. I believe that is why James tells us to "count it all joy when you fall into various trials, knowing that the testing of your faith produces patience" (James 1:2–3 NKJV). When we let patience have its perfect work, we are made complete and lack nothing (vs. 4).

> *"Continuous **effort**— not strength or intelligence—is the key to unlocking our **potential**."*
> —WINSTON CHURCHILL—

God Believes in You!

He believes in you so much He has deposited a portion of His divine potential in you. Even if nobody else in the world believes in you, God does, and with that confidence, you can do whatever He wants you to do.

I encourage you to discover what your potential is and begin developing it. Don't wait until all the conditions are perfect—do something now. Start cultivating the divine seeds of God's ability in you. If you are not sure what they are, find out what you enjoy doing and have natural talents and gifts to do. Begin to train yourself in those areas.

Whatever your gift and calling, entrust it to the Lord, pray for His blessing, and begin to develop it. Remember, your times are in His hands, and He makes all things beautiful in its time. Make a decision right now that you are not going to be satisfied with anything less than all you can be.

resistance to change

Change creates a lot of hard work, requires a lot of creative ideas, and interrupts our regular routine.

In the 1940s, the Swiss watch was the most famous and best quality watch available in the world. About 80 percent of the watches sold worldwide were made in Switzerland. In the late 1950s, the digital watch was presented to the leaders of the Swiss watch company. They rejected this new idea because they *just knew* they already had the best watch and the best watchmakers. They were *sure* their product could not be improved. So the man who developed the digital watch sold the idea to Seiko.

In 1940, Swiss watchmaking companies employed eighty thousand people. Today, they employ eighteen thousand. In 1940, the Swiss sold 80 percent of the world's watches. Today, 80 percent of the watches are digital.

This story of watchmakers represents what happens to people and many organizations: they choose to die rather than choosing to change.

God never changes, but everything else does. In fact, if people and things don't ever change, they are either dead or slowly dying. I believe God has placed a desire and a seed inside each of us for change. We need fresh vision and passion for His purpose for our lives.

Resistance to change is universal. It seizes every generation by the throat and tries to kill all progress. Even though we

" Times change, and so must you. "

crave change, we also fear it. Change threatens us—it takes away what we have become comfortable with. Without change, we don't have to stretch ourselves into new realms. But God wants us to change—He wants us to reach out in faith and let go of the old and take hold of the new.

Change creates hard work, requires creative ideas, and interrupts our regular routine. We naturally fear the unknown, including the fear of failure. We feel safe with old things which have already been proven. When I celebrated my sixtieth birthday, I was very tempted to just say, "It is too late for me to start making all kinds of changes. I think I'll just float along with things the way they have been for the last twenty years."

I am glad I chose not to do that. Today, I feel a fresh fire and a renewed passion like I have not felt in a long time. Jesus said in Matthew 9:17 that new wine could not be poured into old wineskins because the skins would burst and the wine would spill out and be ruined. New wine, which represents a fresh anointing, must be poured into a new wineskin. I am so excited to see what kind of "new wine" God has planned to pour into the "new wineskin" He is directing us to prepare.

Times change, and so must you. Don't get left in the dust!

pursuing
what matters most
Untie your boat from the dock and let

Have you ever thought or even said out loud, "Why am I here? What is my purpose in life?" Many of us have—it's a natural, normal question. Each of us wants to feel we have purpose—we want to know we are accomplishing something and making a difference in the world around us.

Well, you and I can be encouraged to know that God *does* have a purpose for each of our lives. He fills us with His Spirit and positions us here on earth as His representatives. Our purpose is *to do right and glorify God.* When we do right, we bring God glory—we manifest His excellence in a tangible way. Then, when others see it, they want God in their lives too. I believe as we pursue this purpose in life, we will find true contentment, fulfillment, and have all our needs met.

I first need to make it clear that our purpose in life is not the same as the call on our lives—there is a difference. Our call is the *specific job* that God has given us to do, but our purpose is the *reason we are here.* God calls and equips people to be doctors, teachers, homemakers, ministers, and many other types of workers. But our purpose is to do right and glorify God.

the wind of the Holy Spirit take you

out into the deeper waters of life.

Pursuing Our Purpose

"Our purpose is to do right and glorify God."

We pursue our purpose by getting up each day and putting God first. There are many things in life you and I can chase after—job positions, education, relationships, money, material possessions, and so on. But chasing after things will never bring fulfillment. Even if we get them, we end up as empty and unfulfilled as when we began.

God knows what we need and is well aware of our heart's desires. He will grant them if we will just put Him first. Matthew 6:33 says, "But seek (aim at and strive after) first of all His kingdom and His righteousness (His way of doing and being right), and then all these things taken together will be given you besides." What is His kingdom? According to Romans 14:17, the kingdom of God is not about getting a bunch of stuff; it's about knowing that we have been made right with God through Jesus Christ. And in that righteous state, we are able to live right and experience His unshakable peace and abundant joy—regardless our circumstances or what we possess.

Live According to the Word

I believe it is absolutely essential we learn to abandon ourselves to God's care and enjoy where we're at on the way to where we're going. This is one of the most rewarding things God has taught me. Years ago, I thought that everything would be wonderful *if* I didn't have to work, *if* we had more money and a bigger house, *if...if...if.* But when these desires were fulfilled, and I still wasn't happy, I realized the problem was something else. So I asked God what was wrong, and He began to show me that I was a shallow, carnal Christian, living in the superficial realm of what I wanted, thought, and felt. I was expecting God to give me everything I desired, keep me happy all the time, and always explain to me everything that was going on in my life.

I discovered if we want to receive the blessings of God in our lives, we need to live on a deeper level. We need to live according to the Word of God and do what it says—whether or not we feel like it, understand it, want to, or think it's a good idea. We need to be doers of the Word and not hearers only (see James 1:22).

Making the Right Choice

Walking in obedience to God's Word demonstrates our love for Him and puts us in a position to experience the deeper, more abundant life Jesus died to give us (see Joshua 1:8; John 14:15). Moses told the people of Israel exactly what they needed to do to in order to walk in the radical blessings of God: "If you will listen diligently to the voice of the Lord your God, being watchful to do all His commandments which I command you this day, the Lord your God will set you high above all the nations of the earth. And all these blessings shall come upon you and overtake you if you heed the voice of the Lord your God" (Deuteronomy 28:1–2).

> God knows what we need and is well aware of our heart's desires.

This same choice is available to you and me today. Jesus says in Luke 11:28, "Blessed (happy and to be envied) rather are those who hear the Word of God and obey and practice it!" If we want to fulfill our purpose and be blessed, we must make it our aim to know and obey God's commandments. Does this mean we have to be perfect? No. It just means that we are pressing toward the mark of perfection. With all our might, we are *cooperating* with the Holy Spirit and trying to do what is right.

Doing Right Brings Fulfillment

Romans 12:21 says that we overcome evil by doing good. You and I will experience a richer, more meaningful life if we will simply make a decision to do what is right in every situation—whether big or small. This is the principle God wants us to learn: we bring Him glory and put ourselves in a position to be blessed every time we choose to do what's right—even in the seemingly insignificant things. If we will be faithful in little, God will make us ruler over much.

Another way we can bring God glory is in the way we treat people. For starters, we can edify and exhort them. On purpose, we can say things to build them up like: "You're important," "You look nice," "I'm glad you're here," "You're a blessing!" Other ways to be a blessing include believing the best of others, offering forgiveness to those who have offended us, taking time to listen to people, and lending a helping hand when others need it. If we strive to treat everybody we come in contact with like royalty, we will be blessed in the same way. As the Bible says, "Whatsoever a man soweth, that shall he also reap" (Galatians 6:7 KJV).

Gaining a New Perspective

So what are you seeking and pursuing? Don't spend your life chasing after things that have no ability to make you happy. It doesn't matter what you have—if you don't know God's purpose for your life, you have totally missed the boat.

I encourage you to stop living on the basis of what you want, think, and feel. Ask the Holy Spirit to help you make the right choices—they'll bring God glory and be a blessing to you forever. There you will experience true satisfaction and fulfillment and come away with a haul of blessings so big you'll be able to share it with those around you!

"Walking in obedience to God's Word demonstrates our love for Him and puts us in a position to experience the deeper, more abundant life that Jesus died to give us."

finances
& success

Manage Your Time Wisely
& Enjoy Your Life

Do you ever feel like life is passing you by in a blur?

Does it seem as though you're doing a lot of things but

you don't know what you're accomplishing? I've been

there. This is the result of our time managing us

instead of us managing our time. Over the years God

has taught me some very helpful guidelines to show

me how to make the most of the time He's given me.

I believe these keys will be a blessing to you as well.

"Once we know what we are called to do, we need to invest the majority of our time and energy in that thing."

Be a Person of Purpose

One of the first things you and I need to learn is to live our lives *on* purpose and not *off* purpose—to stay focused on what God has called us to do. Ephesians 5:15 says, "Look carefully then how you walk! Live purposefully *and* worthily *and* accurately, not as the unwise *and* witless, but as wise (sensible, intelligent people)." God has a specific call on each of our lives, and He has equipped us with unique gifts and talents to help us carry out that call (see Romans 12:6–8). Once we know what we are called to do, we need to invest the majority of our time and energy in that thing. Now, I don't believe we should be so focused on our plan we are rude to others or that we won't allow the Lord to interrupt it. But we shouldn't be living vague lives—just waiting to see what happens day after day (see Ephesians 5:17). As we stay *on* purpose instead of *off* purpose, we will find both contentment and fulfillment in everything we do.

Give Yourself to Your Gift

It is also important for us to avoid getting entangled in things that we shouldn't be involved in. I believe one of the easiest things to get entangled in is doing *good* things we're not *called* to do. For example, in the early days of my ministry, I became discouraged and frustrated because I couldn't do everything I saw other ministers doing. Thankfully, God showed me He didn't want me to compare myself or compete with other ministers—He just wanted me to be the best *me* I could be.

Any time you and I try to do something we are not called to do, we're going to lose time, waste energy, and end up miserable. Many people are entangled in things they shouldn't be doing, and as a result, their creativity is shut down, and they are not doing *the* thing God has called them to do.

Savor the Flavor of Your Life

Another major revelation that God gave me was that He wants us to take the time to enjoy our lives. Jesus said in John 10:10 He came "that they may have *and* enjoy life, and have it in abundance (to the full, till it overflows)." I was in ministry for many years and didn't enjoy it. But over time God taught me how to slow down and enjoy the things He's blessed me with, like my home, my family, and my finances.

Taking time to enjoy life is like taking time to enjoy a meal. When we eat too fast, we don't get the food's full value or receive the emotional satisfaction we need from eating. The same thing is true with life. If we don't take time to "chew" life, we won't get the "full flavor" out of it. Life is not supposed to be bland and boring—it's supposed to be flavorful and fun.

I encourage you to be a person of purpose and give yourself to your gifting. And by all means, take time to enjoy your life and not just endure it. As you daily surrender your schedule to the Holy Spirit, He will give you the grace to manage your time wisely.

Five Ways to

Most human beings want everything fast, including success, but God is not in a hurry. He is in this with you for the long haul. People who try to fix everything that is wrong in one week often give up. Remember, these changes are supposed to last a lifetime!

TAKE SMALL STEPS

Walking a mile takes about 2,000 steps. There are no other options or shortcuts. And every one of those steps is a tiny success that brings you closer to your goal. The same is true of any other big goal. Your goals need to be broken down into doable steps. Plan your short-term goals so you have something within reach to shoot for. Don't make light of little victories. Small successes breed large ones.

LAUGH AT SETBACKS

No matter how carefully you plan your progress, you will have setbacks. That's part of life. One of the big differences between successful and unsuccessful people is how they respond to those setbacks. Successful people are able to laugh off setbacks and get right back on the horse. Having a bad day does not mean you have a bad life. Remind yourself that ten days forward and one day backward still gets you where you are going.

Make Success Easy

MAKE IT CONVENIENT

If you are a busy person—and who isn't?—you will have to find ways to make your success convenient. And there is no downside to convenience, because it isn't how hard you try; it's the results that matter. For instance, choose a hairstyle and clothing that make you feel good about yourself yet require little maintenance on your part. Choose where you live based on what will be most convenient for you.

MAKE IT FUN

Be realistic. You will keep doing things if you enjoy them. God wants us to enjoy life to the full, and that includes our work. Find a job that fits your call...and that you like to do. If it's something you hate and have to make yourself do, it won't last long term, no matter the money. The goal is to develop a life of spiritual and emotional joy, and that should be part of the payoff all along the way.

REWARD YOURSELF

Don't underestimate the power of rewards. Treating yourself to that new pair of shoes you've wanted may be an appropriate reward that keeps you striving to reach your first short-term goal. Keep the big rewards for meeting your main goals and smaller tokens for your daily positive reinforcements. And remember, it pleases God when you take care of yourself. You are worth it in His eyes.

the importance of

"Well done, good and faithful servant! You have been faithful with a few things; I will put you in charge of many things. Come and share your master's happiness!"—Matthew 25:23 NIV

When it comes to our future, the old adage proves true: *if you and I fail to plan, we plan to fail.* This is true in both the spiritual and natural areas of our lives, particularly regarding the end of our lives. While estate planning may not be your most welcomed topic, it is a vital part of our Christian stewardship.

Now, you may be thinking, *Is this something I need to know?* The answer is yes.

good stewardship

"Seventy percent of Americans do not have a will, and of the remaining 30 percent, 65 percent of the wills are not current."

What Is Stewardship?

By definition, *stewardship* means "the conducting, supervising, or managing of something; the careful and responsible management of something entrusted into one's care." God has entrusted something to each of us—some of us more, and some less based upon the abilities we have. This principle is clearly illustrated in the parable of the talents found in Matthew 25:14–30. As good stewards, you and I are to supervise and manage everything that has been entrusted to us, which includes our time, material possessions, and our financial resources. God is the Owner—we are the stewards, or managers.

What Am I to Do with What God's Entrusted to Me?

There are four basic areas for which we are to make provision. First, which most of us are aware of, we are to provide for God's work—we are to support the spreading of the truth and those who spread it (see Malachi 3:10; Galatians 6:6). Second, we are to provide for our families (1 Timothy 5:8). A third and more general area of responsibility is in managing our overall assets throughout our lifetime as I mentioned earlier. And the fourth area we must take responsibility in is the distribution of our resources at our time of death.

Unfortunately, the United States Treasury shows that 70 percent of Americans do *not* have a will, and of the 30 percent, 65 percent of the wills are not current. Without getting too complicated, a will is nothing more than a written document stating where you desire your resources to go when the Lord takes you home. It is actually the cornerstone of estate planning.

What Is Estate Planning?

Estate planning may sound like something only for those who are well off financially, but that is not the case. The distribution of your possessions after your lifetime is called estate settlement. Deciding in advance *how* your possessions will be distributed is known as estate planning.

If we don't plan our estate, the state will do it for us. Without a will, the laws of the state in which you live will divide your estate, or resources, according to a rigid formula that is not likely to reflect your wishes. The majority goes to probate and the IRS. *Probate* is the costly and time-consuming process of settling your estate, and the *IRS*, of course, is taxes. Yes, the government does a lot of good things, but for every dollar of tax paid, only 24 cents makes it to the actual point of need.

How Can I Be a Wise Steward over What God Has Given Me?

Take time now to plan for your future. Thankfully, the tax codes permit you and me to choose where our assets can go. The truth is, everyone's wealth will go to charity after they die. Believe it or not, probate and the IRS are considered charities. But your family, your church, and other organizations are also viewed as charities, and for every dollar gifted to these charities, about 91 cents makes it to the actual point of need.

So really, the choice is ours. You and I can push off or avoid planning for the future, and the majority of what we've worked for all our life will go toward probate and taxes. Or we can take time now and choose the family members, friends, and organizations we want to see blessed with an inheritance.

Don't allow your life's earnings to be absorbed by the "system." God wants better for His children…and His children's children (see Proverbs 13:22). If you want to be a good steward of all God has entrusted to you, I encourage you to talk with an estate and financial planner and explore your options for the future.

"Loving and being loved is what makes life worth living. Love can melt the hardest heart, heal the wounds of a broken heart, and quiet the fears of an anxious heart. It is a universal language everyone understands. You and I need to learn to love people and use things instead of loving things and using people to get them."

relationships

building solid
relationships

PEOPLE—they are everywhere we go. They come in all shapes and sizes, and we need to learn how to relate to them. The Carnegie Technological Institute has said 90 percent of all people who fail in their life's vocation fail because they cannot get along with people.

Interestingly, the words *relate* and *relationship* are all about *interacting* and *connecting* with others. I believe how we interact and connect with people is very important to God and to a great degree determines the quality of the life we live. Here are a couple of things I have learned over the years which have helped me experience more successful and rewarding relationships.

the ten commandments of human relations

1. **Speak to people.** There is nothing as nice as a cheerful word of greeting.

2. **Smile at people.** It takes seventy-two muscles to frown, only fourteen to smile.

3. **Call people by name.** Music to anyone's ears is the sound of his/her own name.

4. **Be friendly and helpful.**

5. **Be cordial.** Speak and act as if everything you do is genuinely a pleasure, and if it isn't, learn to make it so.

6. **Be genuinely interested in people.** You can like almost everybody if you try.

7. **Be generous with praise,** cautious with criticism.

8. **Be considerate** with the feelings of others. There are usually three sides to a controversy: yours, the other fellow's, and the right one.

9. **Be alert to serve.** What counts most in life is what we do for others.

10. **Add to this a good sense of humor,** a dash of humility, and a big dose of patience, and you will be rewarded many times over through life.

(Adapted from the *Bible Tract Bulletin*)

Stop Trying to Do the Impossible

One of the greatest things you and I can do to have more meaningful relationships is to stop trying to change the people we are in relationship with. This rule holds true for our spouses, children, coworkers, friends, and relatives. People cannot change people. Only God can get inside a person's heart and create a desire for him or her to want to change. If you and I put external pressure on people by making demands on them, it will only result in robbing everyone of peace.

If you are trying to change somebody, stop trying to do something you can do nothing about. Instead, make the situation a matter of prayer. Give your relationship to the Lord, and ask Him to move in the person's life in His timing and in His way. And in the meantime, pray that God will grant you His peace and grace while you wait, helping you learn all He wants you to learn through the situation.

Identify Your Peace Stealers

Another wonderful way to have more rewarding relationships is to identify what steals your peace. In other words, what "rocks your boat" or what "gets your goat?" What does the other person do or not do that really bothers you to the point you lose your peace?

Everyone's "peace stealers" are not alike. There are things that bother me that do not bother Dave. For example, I cannot stand to be in a hurry, and I hate to be late, but Dave tries to do too many things in too little time and we end up

hurrying around the house trying to leave at the last minute. If the enemy can arrange for us to have problems in any of these areas, we begin to lose our peace, and strife enters.

So Satan uses different tactics with each of us to steal our peace and bring strife into our relationships. He sets us up to get us upset. Therefore, you and I must learn to outsmart him (see 2 Corinthians 2:11).

I encourage you to make a list of the things you know steal the peace from your relationships. This is especially good to do with your spouse and children, but it can also be done with a team of coworkers as well as with a close friend. Just sit down and find out what really irritates each of you. Open it up for discussion. Then after each person has shared their heart, go to the Lord in prayer and submit the issues to Him, asking Him for His grace (strength) to avoid doing the things that aggravate and irritate each of you. Do this on an as-needed basis, whenever you sense pressure, tension, or strife coming between you. Take my word for it...this will make a difference, and you will be amazed at the results!

Never Stop Learning

I encourage you to become a student of those you are in relationship with. Instead of always wanting others to understand you, seek to understand them—make it your aim to know where they are coming from and what their heart is. As you take this unselfish approach, the refreshing love of God will

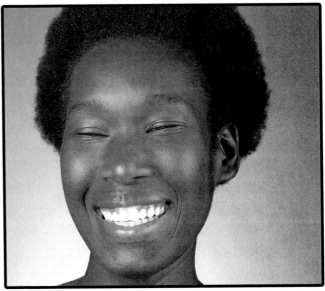

begin to flow, and the oil of the Holy Spirit will remove the friction between you and others. And remember the Golden Rule: "Do to others what you would have them do to you" (Matthew 7:12 NIV). As you invest time, attention, respect, and love into others, God will see to it you reap the same!

forgiveness

"The ability to **forgive** comes from God **and God alone.**"

I believe one of the greatest expressions of love you and I can give is forgiveness. True love between two people—be it husband and wife, parent and child, or two friends—simply says, "I forgive you." There are no exceptions.

Without a doubt, unforgiveness is a major problem—not only in the world but also in the church. It is probably the greatest tool Satan uses to rob us of righteousness, peace, and joy. By holding on to unforgiveness, a root of bitterness can develop in the soul, causing us and others much trouble. That is why God urges us to deal with our anger quickly, strive to live at peace, and accept His grace to deal with the things we face (see Ephesians 4:26–27; Hebrews 12:14–15).

If We Confess Our Sins, He Is Faithful and Just to Forgive Us—1 John 1:9

The ability to forgive comes from God and God alone. It is the core ingredient to every successful relationship, starting with our relationship with the Father. In fact, if we do not repent and confess our sins to God and receive His forgiveness for the wrongs we have done, we have no ability to truly forgive anyone. Without the power of God living in us you and I are powerless to forgive others, for we cannot give away what we do not have. We must first receive forgiveness in order to give it away.

To *forgive* means "to pardon, to overlook an offense and treat the offender as not guilty." And the word *offense* is defined as "a cause or occasion of sin, a stumbling block; something that outrages the moral or physical senses." Every day you and I are faced with a number of opportunities to be offended *or* to walk in love and forgive. If we will go to God, He will give us the grace to forgive.

Take No Account of the Evil Done
—1 Corinthians 13:5

Taking account of a business's financial transactions is a must, but when it comes to the offenses of others, God does not want us to be accountants. He doesn't want us to keep a running record of all the hurtful things others have done to us. When someone takes advantage of us, deceives us, or mistreats us, He wants us to forgive them, let the offense go, and move forward with life (see Philippians 3:13). Now, I realize some offenses are harder to let go of than others. Forgiving the people who verbally, emotionally, and sexually abused me while I was growing up was not an overnight thing. It took time. But it all started with a willingness to let go of the past and release those who mistreated me.

God doesn't want us to keep a **running record** of all the **hurtful things** others have done to us.

Be Not Wise in Your Own Eyes—Proverbs 3:7

One thing that will help us stop taking an account of people's offenses is to give up our "right" to be right. In other words, we are willing to be wrong, even if we are certain we are right. This is walking in love. The truth is, there are times when you and I think we are right, but we are really wrong.

For instance, over the years I've often been certain I knew the directions to somewhere despite Dave's questionings, only to be absolutely wrong. After scenarios like this played out over and over, God brought me to the point where I became more open-minded to other people's ideas and realized it is not worth arguing over who is right. These experiences can be humiliating, but sometimes they are the only way to crucify our pride and develop humility.

Now, I have learned to say, "Well, Dave, I think this is the way, but I have been wrong before." This mind-set has helped me keep my peace and avoid getting into strife with not only my husband but also others (see 2 Timothy 2:23).

Forgive as the Lord Forgave You
—Colossians 3:13

"Love is the only force that will override hatred, anger, bitterness, and unforgiveness."

Forgiving others serves two main purposes: to give to someone who has offended us and then asks us to forgive him, and to offer to a person who did not intend to offend us and does not know they did. We need to forgive them in order to remain at peace ourselves and keep the flow of God's forgiveness and power coming to us.

Jesus explained this principle through the parable of the servant who owed his king a tremendous amount of money but could not pay it back. Moved with compassion from the servant's plea for mercy, the king forgave the man and canceled his debt completely. This same servant found a man who owed him a much smaller debt, and the man begged for mercy, but the servant was unwilling to forgive. When the king found out, he called in his servant who was unwilling to forgive and said, "I forgave *and* cancelled all that [great] debt of yours because you begged me to. And should you not have had pity *and* mercy on your fellow attendant, as I had pity *and* mercy on you? And in wrath his master turned him over to the torturers (the jailors), till he should pay all that he owed. So also My heavenly Father will deal with every one of you if you do not freely forgive your brother from your heart *his offenses*" (Matthew 18:32–35).

If we choose not to forgive others for their offenses and mistreatment, God cannot and will not forgive us. As hard as this sounds, it is true (see Matthew 6:12; Mark 11:26).

Whenever You Pray, if You Have Anything Against Anyone, Forgive Him—Mark 11:25

Now, you may be thinking, *Joyce, I made a decision to forgive, but the thoughts of how this person hurt me won't seem to go away.* Let me share this story I believe will help you. Corrie ten Boom, a survivor of the Holocaust, told of not being able to forget a wrong done to her. She forgave the person, but she kept rehashing the incident and was unable to sleep. Finally, Corrie cried out to God for help in putting the problem to rest. She said, "His help came in the form of a kindly Lutheran pastor to whom I confessed my failure after two sleepless weeks."

"Up in the church tower," he said, nodding out the window, "is a bell which is rung by pulling on a rope. But you know what? After the sexton lets go of the rope, the bell keeps on swinging. First ding, then dong. Slower and slower until there's a final dong and it stops. I believe the same thing is true of forgiveness. When we forgive, we take our hand off the rope. But if we've been tugging at our grievances for a long time, we mustn't be surprised if the old angry thoughts keep coming for a while. They're just the ding-dongs of the old bell slowing down."

If you have not been able to forgive someone who seriously hurt you, it may be you have allowed the enemy to deceive you into believing you cannot forgive them. If so, I encourage you to make this declaration daily:

I can and will forgive _____ for hurting me. I can do it because God's Spirit lives in me and enables me to forgive. Father, please heal the wounds in my soul that have resulted from being hurt and holding on to the hurt. In Jesus' name, Amen.

Remember, love is the only force that will override hatred, anger, bitterness, and unforgiveness. It is not a feeling—it is a decision. Don't open a door for the devil to torment you by holding on to past hurts. Let them go. God's love is free, and as we have freely received His love, we must freely give His love...especially in the form of forgiveness.

Find a New Way to Walk in Love

"Loving ourselves and loving others is not an option or a suggestion—it's a commandment."

Among all the things I teach, walking in love is definitely one of my favorites. Why? Because everything about our Christian walk is founded on and grows out of love. Love begins with God and ends with others: God loves us, we accept His love, we begin to love Him back, and then we allow His love to flow through us to other people. This completes the cycle. If we don't receive His love, we cannot love Him or others—we can't give away what we don't have. I know because I tried to love others for years and failed because I didn't love myself. But after I meditated on scriptures confirming God's love and repeatedly told myself God loves me and accepts

me, His love for me became a reality, and I was able to start loving others.

It's important to understand that loving ourselves and loving others is not an option or a suggestion—it's a commandment. Jesus said, "A new command I give to you: Love one another. As I have loved you, so you must love one another" (John 13:34 NIV). People are starved for love, and we are the instruments through which God wants to give it to them. We can't wait for a feeling to motivate us to start loving others. Love is not a *feeling*—it is *action*. It is a set of behaviors we *choose* to operate in—an effort you and I do *on purpose*.

How Can We Understand Love?

"This is how we've come to understand and experience love: Christ sacrificed his life for us. This is why **we ought to live sacrificially for our fellow believers**, and not just be out for ourselves" (1 John 3:16 The Message). That's what real love is all about—living a life of self-denial. You and I cannot walk in love and be selfish and self-centered. We must make a daily choice to get our minds off ourselves—our wants, our needs, what we've done wrong, what we've done right, etc.—and focus on others. Now, this doesn't mean we abandon caring for ourselves. It just means we're always open to helping others and are actually looking for ways to be a blessing.

What's the Alternative to Walking in Love?

A meaningless, self-centered life which is dead—yes, dead—is the alternative to walking in love. First John 3:14 says, "The way we know we've been transferred from death to life is that we love our brothers and sisters. Anyone who doesn't love is as good as **dead**" (The Message). Now, this is not talking about not breathing, but rather about living a joyless, empty existence. I remember living like that many years ago—walking around miserable, depressed, unfulfilled, and upset all the time. I had no joy, no peace, and no righteousness, because all I cared about was myself. The truth is, we can't keep God's love all to ourselves bottled up inside. We have to let it out, and we do that through our words and our actions.

In Order for God's Love to Grow, It Has to Flow

After we learn to love ourselves, the next group of people we're told to love are those of the household of faith—our brothers and sisters in Christ. First John 3:17 says, "If you see some brother or sister in need and have the means to do something about it but turn a cold shoulder and do nothing, what happens to God's love? It disappears. And you made it disappear" (The Message). What does it mean to make God's love disappear? It means we withhold, or hold back, His tangible presence from being seen and felt by those around us. You and I can have a right heart or good intentions, but if we don't *act* on what we're feeling in our spirit, our witness is more or less worthless. As James 2:17 says, faith without works is dead.

God expects us to treat everybody well and to put other people's needs before ours so they can see and feel Him. When we walk in love, we bring Him glory—we manifest His excellence out in the open. As 1 John 4:8 says, "God is love." So when we show God's love to others, God's presence is there. Every time we give someone a compliment, open a door, share a smile, offer patience, or make a sacrifice to make somebody else happy, **God is there** (see 1 John 4:12).

This reminds me of a true story I ran across while writing this article. A newspaper columnist and minister named George Crane told a story of a woman who came into his office full of hatred toward her husband. She told him, "I do not only want to get rid of him; I want to get even. Before I divorce him, I want to hurt him as much as he has me."

Dr. Crane suggested an ingenious plan. He said, "Go home and act as if you really love your husband. Tell him how much he means to you. Praise him for every decent trait. Go out of your way to be as kind, considerate, and generous as possible. Spare no efforts to please him and enjoy him. Make him believe you love him. After you've convinced him of your undying love and that you cannot live without him, 'drop the bomb.' Tell him that you're getting a divorce. That will really hurt him."

"I had no joy, no peace, and no righteousness, because all I cared about was myself."

"This is how we've come to
understand and experience love:
Christ sacrificed his life for us. This
is why we ought to live sacrificially for our
fellow believers, and not just be
out for ourselves."

—1 John 3:16 The Message

With revenge in her eyes, she smiled and exclaimed, "Beautiful, beautiful. Will he ever be surprised!" And she went home and enthusiastically heeded his advice, acting "as if" she loved him. For two months she showed him love and kindness—listening, giving, reinforcing, and sharing.

When she didn't return, Dr. Crane called her and asked, "Are you ready now to go through with the divorce?"

"Divorce?" she exclaimed. "Never! I discovered I really do love him." Amazingly, her actions had changed her feelings. Dr. Crane said *motion* resulted in *emotion*—her ability to love was established not so much by fervent promise as by repeated deeds. And I can tell you from experience that the same thing will happen to you.

So Why Do We Walk in Love?

We do it for God—not for us. We belong to Him, we live for Him, and we're His representatives. We choose to walk in love because Jesus said to. But as this true story illustrates, when we do choose to walk in love, we can't help but be blessed too.

romantic ideas

for Her

- Hire a maid to clean the house one month.
- Take her car for a thorough washing and detailing.
- Take her on a "Scavenger Hunt Date" at the mall, giving her the challenge of buying a certain number of items under a certain dollar amount—you provide the money. Then take her to a restaurant.
- Make her some coupons and include one for a neck and back massage, a day off from cooking, and a Saturday afternoon to herself.

for Him

- Plan a date for the two of you to do one of his favorite activities (i.e., bowling, skating, fishing, hiking, etc.).
- Hide little love notes in his car, lunch, coat pocket, and desk.
- Plan a candlelight dinner at home for the two of you, complete with soft music and his favorite food.
- Get him that new power tool, music CD, or book he's been wanting.

marriage
& family

to enjoy life to the full, keep it simple

simplicity
loving God & enjoying life

MOST OF US occasionally like to invite people over to our homes. But every once in a while, we invite people over and don't enjoy their visit. Why is that? Is it because, like the following illustration of Martha, we turn that simple time of fellowship into something it should not be?

"Jesus entered a certain village, and a woman named Martha received *and* welcomed Him into her house. And she had a sister named Mary, who seated herself at the Lord's feet and was listening to His teaching. But Martha [overly occupied and too busy] was distracted with much serving; and she came up to Him and said, Lord, is it nothing to You that my sister has left me to serve alone? Tell her then to help me [to lend a hand and do her part along with me]! But the Lord replied to her by saying, Martha, Martha, you are anxious and troubled about many things; there is need of only one or *but a few things*. Mary has chosen the good portion [that which is to her advantage], which shall not be taken away from her" (Luke 10:38–42).

I have noticed that complicated people like Martha and me get burned out easily because we tend to make everything so much harder than it ought to be.

Why Can't I Keep It Simple?

"Do you need to be more like Mary and less like Martha?"

In the earlier days of my married life, I might have said to a group of friends, "Why don't you come over Sunday after church? We'll throw some hot dogs on the grill and open up some potato chips and some pork and beans. I'll make some tea, and we'll have some good fellowship."

They would have said, "Okay. We'll come; that sounds like fun."

Well, that would seem to be easy and something I could do without a lot of fuss and bother. But I just couldn't leave it alone. The hot dogs would become steaks, and the potato chips potato salad. If I invited six people, I would start thinking about the twelve I didn't invite who might get upset if they knew the six were coming, and soon eighteen people were coming over. We would have to buy lawn furniture, which we couldn't afford, paint the barbecue pit, wax all the floors, and plant new flowers. Eventually, I would become angry with everyone in the house because I had to work so hard trying to prepare for the party. A simple barbeque turned into a nightmare.

Why couldn't I just keep it simple? I had an ungodly need to impress everyone. I did have a problem, but it was one *I* created. Instead of worrying and fretting, I needed to learn to simplify my plans, lighten up, and enjoy life!

Simple Ways to Simplify

I believe life should be a celebration. Far too many believers don't even enjoy life, let alone celebrate it. Many people truly love Jesus Christ and are on their way to heaven, but very few are enjoying the trip.

May I share with you with all the love I know how to muster? If you are having problems with your life, it may be because you are creating many of them yourself. You may be taking things which could be simple, fun, easy, and even inexpensive, and complicating them. Then you probably get mad at everyone around you because you are frustrated.

People do the same thing at holidays. They get into major debt trying to buy presents because they are afraid of what people will think if they don't give them gifts. If you really don't have the money, just tell people you can't afford to buy presents this year. Truth is simple. Life gets complicated when we try to ignore and hide the truth.

Some of us have so much stuff we can hardly walk through our homes. When I first realized my need for simplicity, I became acutely aware that every knickknack I was tempted to buy would soon be just one more thing I would have to dust at home. You can have life-changing joy if you simplify your everyday life.

If you want to live a less-complicated life, you may have to simplify it by not doing so much. Most people who are stressed and frustrated have become burned out because they try to squeeze too much into their schedules. So learn to say no to what you don't want to do. And learn to say yes to what is really important. Don't allow your joy to be stolen by being so busy you have no time to enjoy all God has given you—your spouse, your children, your grandkids, and your friends.

"To enjoy life

to the full,

keep it simple."

Believing Simplifies Life

Jesus came to simplify your life; Satan wants to complicate your life. Religion teaches you to juggle the many tasks of Bible reading, prayer, fasting, memorizing spiritual songs, and doing good deeds. Just when you think you're doing all right, the devil throws you a new requirement to work into your routine.

Decide not to live like that anymore. I tried to do all the things I thought I had to do to keep God happy, but God wasn't asking me to do most of it. I was just following other people. I thought I should do what they were doing because they were being blessed. Following people instead of God is another tool the devil uses to distract us from God's simple plan for our lives. I lived under the tyranny of self-inflicted "oughts and shoulds." Life gets complicated when we think we always have to do something.

Living a complicated lifestyle will steal your joy, but simplicity will bring power and peace. It may be difficult to do, but you can learn to have a simple approach to everything. It begins by accepting the simplicity that is yours in Christ Jesus (2 Corinthians 11:3). Being uncomplicated simply means trusting God. Trust releases both peace and joy, as well as the blessings of God, and it is the key to enjoying every single day of your life.

Achieve
the Marriage
of Your Dreams

WE ALL WANT MARRIAGE to be a triumph, not a tragedy. But Satan wants a tragedy, and we need to be increasingly aware of the subtle ways he tries to destroy our marriages and home lives.

There's nothing better than a really good marriage and nothing worse than a bad one. Whether you are married for thirty days or thirty years, the time is right to discover how you can transform your marriage to be all God intends it to be. Whether you are suffering through a marriage crisis or simply want to improve your marriage, you'll find hope and courage in God's promises of healing and restoration.

No matter what you may be feeling about your marriage at this moment, God wants to release His power on you and your spouse and guide you along the path to the marriage of your dreams. After all, the abundant life He promised is meant for your marriage too!

Where You Started Is Not Where You Need to End

Many people enter a marriage because they're expecting the other person to do something for them, to give them something, to "make me happy." But we need to look at marriage from the standpoint of giving, not getting. When each partner fully gives him or herself over to the thought, *What can I do for you?* each will receive everything desired—and more.

The Bible says, "It is more blessed to give than to receive" (Acts 20:35 KJV), and "Let marriage be held in honor (esteemed worthy, precious, of great price, and especially dear) in all things" (Hebrews 13:4). It took me a long time to learn the meaning of these verses.

One morning, as I sat in my pajamas praying, the Lord said to me, "Joyce, I really can't do anything else in your life until you do what I told you to do concerning your husband." He had been dealing with me because I was having problems with my attitude toward Dave.

After praying, I got up and went to take a shower in the *new bathroom Dave had just installed.* Since he had not yet put up a towel rack, I laid my towel on the toilet seat and started to step into the shower. Dave saw what I was doing and asked me, "Why did you put your towel there?"

Right away I could feel my emotions getting stirred up. "What's wrong with putting it there?" I asked in a sarcastic tone.

As an engineer, Dave answered with typical mathematical logic. "Well, since we don't have a floor mat yet, if you put your towel in front of the shower door, when you get out you won't drip water on the carpet while reaching for it."

"Well, what difference would it make if I did get a little water on the carpet?" I asked in a huff.

As it turned out, I did what Dave suggested, but I did it by throwing the towel onto the floor in a rage. It was three full days before I calmed down. I was the noisy gong and clanging cymbal described in 1 Corinthians 13.

> "Loving sacrifice means that you are not going to have your way all the time."

A good marriage does not just happen, no matter how wildly in love you were when you got married. Love is the highest form of maturity, and it often requires a sacrificial gift. Sacrifice means you are not going to have your way all the time. Even a mediocre marriage requires sacrifice. It is important to understand that true love gives of itself. This means both the husband and wife are called to love each other with unconditional love. There has to be a sacrifice of selfish desires if a couple is going to enjoy a triumphant marriage.

Becoming One Flesh Is a Process that Takes Time

God said marriage will bring two people together and cause them to *become one flesh* (see Genesis 2:24). The blending of two individuals into one harmonious marriage is a process that takes time. Making a relationship work is hard and sometimes even painful. Doing what God says to do is not always easy, but obeying God has greater rewards than I could have ever expected.

The Bible says we are supposed to be in agreement. There are no two people who are in a more important position to get in agreement than a married couple. Most marital problems include strife from communication problems, sexual misunderstanding, money, goals, and parenting.

> Choose to have a good marriage every day.

Many wars are started in our homes over nitpicky things that don't make any difference at all. If you want to have power in your marriage and in your prayer life, you have to get along.

So how do two people with very different personalities—who don't think alike, who don't feel the same about a lot of things, who don't even like the same kind of food—learn to agree? Agreement comes when the people involved stop being selfish. A lot of adults still deal with selfishness. All selfishness amounts to is, "I want what I want when I want it, and I don't really care what you want because I want what I want." Selfishness is an immature inward focus.

If each one of us will learn to voice our wants but choose what best serves everybody in the family, we will find peace. The key is to care about what the other person needs and be willing to humble ourselves to the point we don't have to be right all the time and do what we can to meet those needs. You can learn how to "disagree agreeably" without causing strife.

Enjoy Each Other

You can have such fun in your marriage when you begin to agree with each other. Do you know God did not put you together to be miserable? He didn't put you together to fight, pick on each other, or try and change each other. The Bible says a

woman is to enjoy her husband. Think about that. I rarely hear a woman say, "You know what? I really enjoy my husband." And God wants us to enjoy each other. He wants us to have fun together.

Seriously, couples need to take every opportunity available in a day to laugh. Seize the moment and make each other laugh about something. I was always so serious, somber, and a deep thinker, always trying to solve some problem. I've learned in recent years to be more childlike and lighthearted.

Your husband needs a helpmate, not a nag, a boss, a critic, a teacher, or a potter who wants to keep reworking him on the wheel all the time. He doesn't need you to be a personal advisor, unless he asks for it. But he does need a friend and a place to come home where he is championed, in spite of what he had to put up with through his day. He may not want to relive the stresses he went through at

work by telling you about it, but he certainly will enjoy your warm embrace when he comes home. Help him to realize there is more to life than what he experienced at work.

Commitment Is the Adhesive of Marriage

Marriage begins with a promise between a man and a woman to honor and cleave to each other for life. Too many couples depend on love to keep their marriage together, but commitment is the adhesive of marriage, and love is the reward of keeping the promise to stand beside each other through both good and bad times, in both sickness and in health, in both poverty and wealth. The process of keeping the promise is what makes love grow between the two of them.

Choose to have a good marriage every day. Don't leave that one for chance to decide!

"Raising a child is an awesome responsibility that many people take on without proper preparations."

Discovering God's Plan for Parenting

As parents, God has given us unique authority and influence over our children—but with it comes tremendous responsibility. Parenting is one of the most difficult—and important—challenges we experience in life, and we're foolish if we think we will automatically know how to be good parents.

The Bible has much to say about children and how we as parents are to care for them. But the information it provides is useless unless we study it and put it into practice. I know. I've been there and made many mistakes. But as I grew and matured in my spiritual life, God began to show me a better way.

Parents Are Personal Trainers

One of the most commonly quoted scriptures about parenting is Proverbs 22:6: "Train up a child in the way he should go [and in keeping with his individual gift or bent], and when he is old he will not depart from it." This verse clearly says it is the parents' responsibility to discover God's will with regard to what is best for their children—keeping in mind their personal gifts and tendencies. We are to train our children in the way they should go—that means the way *God* wants them to go...not the way *we* want. We are to pray and seek God's will for their lives. Then we are to observe the personalities, strengths, and weaknesses of our children, and do what we can to help them become all that God wants them to be. This takes time and patience.

Be Wise with Your Words

We must be very careful about the words we say to and *about* our kids. Our words are important tools that can be used to build them up or tear them down. Always stay away from saying negative and downgrading statements to your children. Saying phrases such as "You *never* do anything right" can damage a child's confidence...and even change the course of his or her life.

It is sometimes necessary to tell our children what they do wrong, but it is also important to tell them what they do *right*. When correcting your children, separate their behavior from who they are. Tell them what they *did* was bad, but assure them *they* are not bad. Verbalize your love for them and assure them they have tremendous potential. Always speak words that instill hope in the hearts of your children (see Jeremiah 29:11). Speak to your children the way you would like others to speak to you (see Matthew 7:12).

Hope in the God of Restoration

Many people feel inadequate as parents...or that they have already made so many mistakes their relationships with their children have been ruined. But I want you to know God is a God of restoration, and if you'll ask Him, He will bring healing to your relationships with your children.

Follow God's instructions and be patient. Take each season of parenting as it comes and lean heavily on God to help you. Do your best, but don't get down on yourself if you're not perfect. Jesus died for all—including imperfect parents—and He stands in the gap for our weaknesses and makes up the difference. If we will seek and obey Him, we can learn to do all things according to the leading of His Spirit—and parenting is no exception. Do your best to follow God's parenting plan, and during the process, be sure to *enjoy your children*!

balanced
living

It's OK to Lighten Up!

Are you often agitated, uptight, or anxious? That was me "to a tee" years ago. I lived my life so intensely I couldn't really enjoy anything. I was plagued with anxiety—most of the time for no apparent reason. I desperately wanted to be happy, but I had no clue what to do.

The Word of God teaches us that "anxiety in a man's heart weighs it down" (see Proverbs 12:25), and this is so true. Many people go through life with the weight of the world on their shoulders—upset, disturbed, and tied in knots on the inside, overwhelmed with trying to take care of themselves. Satan, our enemy, wants us to stay that way. Why? To keep our attention off the good things God has given us to keep us from enjoying our relationship with the Lord and the abundant life He died to give us.

Understand the Problem

The first step in dealing with anxiety is knowing what anxiety is. *Anxiety* is "apprehensiveness or worry about what may happen; concern about a possible future event." The Lord once showed me that anxiety is caused by trying to mentally and emotionally get

into things that haven't happened yet or things that have already been. In other words, anxiety is mentally leaving where you are and getting into an area of the past or the future.

Ever since the Lord impressed that upon me, I have made it my goal to lighten up and enjoy my life. There are many serious things going on in the world around us, but we need to learn to relax and take things as they come without getting nervous or upset about them. In spite of the turmoil and trouble around us, our daily confession should be, "This is the day the Lord has made; I WILL rejoice and be glad in it!" (Psalm 118:24).

Be a Now Person

One of the greatest causes of anxiety is our failure to live in today. Many people spend too much time replaying past failures in their minds or being anxious about future events that may or may not take place. I know because I used to do it. However, God wants you and me to learn to live in today—to be a now person.

Ecclesiastes 5:1 makes this principle clear. It says, "Keep your foot [give your

"Worry pulls tomorrow's cloud over today's sunshine."

—CHARLES SWINDOLL

mind to what you are doing]." In other words, you and I need to keep our footing or maintain balance in our lives. We must learn to focus on what we are presently doing and not what we already did or what we are going to do. If we don't, we will end up being anxious and worried because we will always be mentally dealing with yesterday or tomorrow when we should be living today.

I like what my friend John Maxwell says: "Yesterday ended last night, and you can't depend on tomorrow. Today is the only time you have." I believe there is an anointing on today. Jesus referred to Himself as "I Am" (John 8:58). He did not refer to Himself as "I Was" or "I Will Be," and that is because He is always in the present. He doesn't want us to be anxious or worried about tomorrow. Clearly, He says, "Do not worry *or* be anxious about tomor-

row, for tomorrow will have worries *and* anxieties of its own. Sufficient for each day is its own trouble" (Matthew 6:34).

You and I do not need to be anxious about next week, next month, or next year. We need to give our full attention to today. God will give us the grace (ability, strength, power) we need to live today…today. He is not going to give us tomorrow's grace until tomorrow. The next time you begin to lose your peace and get anxious about something in the past or the future, ask the Lord to help you refocus your thinking on what is going on today. Yes, learn from the past and prepare for the future, but live in the present.

Focus on the Good

Another cause of anxiety is not being content with where we are or with what God is doing in our lives. When I first started out in ministry, I had a big dream—a dream of teaching large crowds. I was so anxious to see my dream become reality I began saying, "I'll be so glad when I have hundreds in my meetings." Then when hundreds were attending, I said, "I'll be glad when I have a thousand." But when we hit a thousand and I still wasn't happy, I knew something wasn't right. I began to realize outward circumstances don't bring true, lasting joy.

To live in the fullness of the joy of the Lord, you and I must find something to be glad about besides our current circumstances. We must learn to get our joy from the Lord living inside us instead of what is happening outside us. Remember the song "He Has Made Me Glad"? That is the key. During those early days, I sang it more like, "If He does what I want Him to do, He has made me glad; if He doesn't, He has made me sad." Thankfully, the Lord taught me that the fullness of joy is found in His *presence*—not His *presents* (see Psalm 16:11).

You and I must guard against spending our lives waiting to be glad and learn to be glad now. Unlike circumstances and people, Jesus Christ is unchangeable—always the same (see Hebrews 13:8). As we learn to focus on Him and His goodness, His love, His provision, and His friendship, His joy will be released inside us.

I believe this is what Paul is saying in Philippians 4:4. From inside a prison, he boldly declared, "Rejoice in the Lord always [delight, gladden yourselves in Him]; again I say, Rejoice!" Then in verses six and seven, he gives us a proven prescription for overcoming anxiety: "Don't worry about anything; instead, pray about everything. Tell God what you need, and thank him for all he has done. Then you will experience God's peace, which exceeds anything we can understand. His peace will guard your hearts and minds as you live in Christ Jesus" (NLT).

Notice that we are to rejoice *in* everything, not *after* everything is over. Paul goes on to say we are to bring our anxious thoughts and feelings to the Lord as soon as they come—whenever they come. We are to tell Him what we need and thank Him for how He helped us before. Recalling the details of how God helped us when our situation seemed hopeless increases our faith—it magnifies the Lord and minimizes the problem. As we learn to practice this prescription, God's peace will be released in our lives.

Be Your Best

"Cast your burden on the Lord [releasing the weight of it] and He will sustain you; He will never allow the [consistently] righteous to be moved (made to slip, fall, or fail)."—Psalm 55:22

Cast Your Cares

God loves you, and He wants you to be at peace. Jesus said in John 14:27, "Peace I leave with you; My [own] peace I now give *and* bequeath to you. Not as the world gives do I give to you. Do not let your hearts be troubled, neither let them be afraid. [Stop allowing yourselves to be agitated and disturbed; and do not permit yourselves to be fearful and intimidated and cowardly and unsettled.]"

How do you stop allowing yourself to be anxious, agitated, and unsettled? By developing the healthy habit of living today, by bringing your anxious thoughts and feelings to God as soon as they come, and by casting your cares upon Him. First Peter 5:7 says you are to cast "the whole of your care [all your anxieties, all your worries, all your concerns, once and for all] on Him, for He cares for you affectionately *and* cares about you watchfully."

Just go to God and say, "Father, I am anxious about [whatever is weighing on your heart]. Lord, if there is anything I can do in this situation, please show me. You have been so faithful to me in the past...[say aloud how God helped you]. I am so grateful You care for me and watch over me. I give You these cares because they are too heavy for me to hold. As You helped me before, I believe You will help me again. Release Your peace in my life right now to drive away the anxiety and worry coming against me. I receive it by faith—in Jesus' name, Amen."

God Almighty, Creator of the universe, cares intensely for YOU. He is mindful of you. You are indelibly tattooed on the palms of His hands, and His thoughts about you and toward you are countless. I encourage you to cast your cares on Him. Whenever you begin to feel anxious, run to Him in prayer. Exchange your anxiety for His peace. It really is okay to lighten up!

the Sweet Satisfaction of Contentment

One of the characteristics of true joy is contentment, and if there is any quality people in the world today deeply desire and yet are missing, it's contentment. Even among Christians, feelings of discontentment and dissatisfaction dominate the lives of many. But this is not God's will. He wants us to find contentment in Him and

Are You Content?

Webster's 1828 dictionary defines *content* as "rest or quietness of the mind in the present condition; satisfaction which holds the mind in peace, restraining complaint, opposition, or further desire, and often implying a moderate degree of happiness."

One of the benefits of living in God's kingdom is the privilege of being content and satisfied even when our circumstances are undesirable. First Timothy 6:6 says "godliness accompanied with contentment (that contentment which is a sense of inward sufficiency) is great *and* abundant gain." The truth is, *contentment is worth more than all the material possessions you and I could possibly accumulate in a lifetime.* Nothing we have or will obtain is worth anything if we are not satisfied inside.

I believe contentment is a decision to be happy with what we have, right where we are. Now, this doesn't mean we have to accept everything that's going on in our lives and never want change. It's good to want things to improve in ourselves, in others, and in the world around us. But while we're hoping for better days, we can learn to enjoy where we are on the way to where we're going. If we don't learn to enjoy today, we'll never get a second chance at enjoying it.

A Major Cause of Discontentment

I believe many people are discontented because they're trying to live outside their call in life. There are a large number of people who think they must become what

"When you and I come to the place where we say, 'Lord, I only want what You want me to have,' we will find true peace and contentment. There is no other way."

another person is, and that kind of thinking will steal your joy. I know because I experienced it firsthand.

It was so liberating to me when I finally discovered I didn't have to be like anyone else. Before then, I thought I had to be like my husband, who was always so patient, or like my pastor's wife, who was soft-spoken and gentle.

But thankfully, I learned that all God requires of me is to be the best "me" He created me to be. He has called me to be a mouthpiece to the body of Christ, and along with the call, He has given me the gifts I need to fulfill it. The Bible says in Romans 12:6 that each of us has been given specific gifts according to the grace, which is God-given power and ability, to fulfill our call in life. As long as you and I try to be someone we're not or try to fulfill a call not our own, we will be continually discontent.

God rewards those who follow an obedient lifestyle—especially obedience to the specific calling He has placed on our lives. If we will just do what God is asking us to do and be the people He made us to be, His rewards will literally chase us down and flood our lives (see Deuteronomy 28:1–2).

Developing Contentment in Our Souls

First, you and I need to realize that being content is something we learn over time and through experience. The apostle Paul says in Philippians 4:12, "I've learned by now to be quite content whatever my circumstances. I'm just as happy with little as with much, with much as with little. I've found the recipe for being happy whether full or hungry, hands full or hands empty" (The Message).

I don't know how long it took Paul to learn that Christ was sufficient for all his needs. But somehow, he finally learned to be content, and we can learn too. No matter what state we're in, we can learn to be content whether we have a lot or a little. Christ will empower us to be ready for anything (see Philippians 4:13).

We usually learn to be content as a result of living discontented lives for a long period of time and then crying out to God for His intervention. When I was sick of being constantly dissatisfied with my life, I went to God and said, "Lord, I don't want to live in this misery any longer. Getting this thing or having that thing is not worth it. Just give me what You want me to have because unless You want me to have it, I don't want it."

Overcome the Struggle to Be Content

I encourage you to get into the Word for yourself and find some specific scriptures to renew your mind and help you develop the contentment that is yours through Christ. As the writer of Psalm 131:2 wrote, begin to declare, "I have calmed and quieted my soul; like a weaned child with his mother, like a weaned child is my soul within me [ceased from fretting]." The power of life and death is in our tongue, and God wants you to begin calling those things that don't currently exist as if they already did. In time, you will see them come to pass (see Proverbs 18:21; Romans 4:17).

God loves you and has designed only the best for you. I challenge you to begin saying, "I am happy with what God is doing in my life. I don't want what anybody else has because I probably wouldn't be able to handle it if I had it. I only want what God wants me to have. I believe He is going to give it to me, but only *if* and *when* it is right for me to have it."

Remember, contentment and joy do not come from trying to undertake things that aren't God's will for you, and, therefore, aren't within your God-given talents and abilities to accomplish. That is not a negative confession—it is godly wisdom. Become content with the wonderful person God made you to be, and your level of contentment and joy will improve dramatically!

"Real contentment and joy come from remaining within the boundaries of what God has called and equipped you to do."

Be your best!
Joyce

Excerpt from Joyce Meyer and Deborah Bedford's Novel

The Penny

CHAPTER ONE: There are two things I will always remember about summers in St. Louis. One is walking barefoot on pavement so hot that I could pop the tar bubbles with my toes. Pavement so hot that, by the end of July, the hide on the soles of my feet was as thick as my tanned-leather coin purse from Woolworth's and I could cross Arsenal Street without having to run. Every year, some photographer from the *Post-Dispatch* would take a shot of an egg frying sunny-side up on the sidewalk and the paper would run it on the front page. HOT ENOUGH TO FRY AN EGG ON THE SIDEWALK! the headline would bellow. As if they were telling us something we didn't already know.

The other thing I'll always remember is the summer of the penny. At this point in my life, I'm picking up pennies all the time. But that wasn't the case back then. Not before *the* penny, the *important* penny, the one that led

me to Miss Shaw at the jewelry store.

I learned from that first special penny how important the little things in life can be.

Because the penny led me to knowing Miss Shaw, and knowing Miss Shaw was what started things changing between Daddy and Jean and Mama and me.

Before the penny, if you'd have asked what I knew about Miss Shaw, I'd have shrugged and acted like you were loony. "I don't know *anything* about her," I would've told you, because girls like me had no reason to speak with ladies like Miss Shaw.

No one in the neighborhood knew much about Miss Shaw. For although my one friend, Marianne Thompson, and I had seen her greet her customers with a warm smile like she could tell something special about them, people like us never had any reason to set foot inside a jewelry store. So Marianne and I just wondered among ourselves, did she come from money or did she earn it? Did she grow up around here? How old was she? How did she manage to keep her hair dry on rainy days without using an umbrella? Why didn't she get wet hair on a rainy day? And because of that, because no one knew where she'd come from or who her parents were or how she'd come to buy her own jewelry store, she was the most profound mystery along Grand Avenue. And you know how everybody likes to talk about a mystery.

"Now there's a woman up to no good," Daddy would comment whenever he happened to see Miss Shaw promenading along the sidewalk downtown with her pocketbook tucked beneath her arm. Daddy had a general distrust for all things to do with women bettering themselves. And he had a healthy contempt for Miss Shaw in particular. "That woman causes all the talk, anyway. She *thrives* on being talked about, or else she wouldn't stay tight-mouthed the way she does. Let me tell you, there's a woman who rides a high horse. Acting like the rest of us aren't good enough to know her."

Only one part of the neighborhood hearsay going around about Miss Shaw didn't match up with the stories of Miss Shaw's grace, beauty, and superiority. Marianne Thompson made a vow to me once that she'd seen Miss Shaw sneaking around in the shadows of the town cemetery. She'd been hiding behind trees, Marianne insisted, and taking careful steps through the fallen leaves so as not to make any sound with her high-heeled shoes, and glancing around stealthily to make certain nobody saw her. She'd been looking around for a grave, Marianne said, and when she found the one she was looking for, it didn't have a stone. Marianne had seen Miss Shaw stoop to the ground and wipe the dead leaves from a smooth patch of dirt and place her gloved hand atop the dry mound. She held her hand to the ground for the longest time, Marianne declared, like she expected to feel a heartbeat.

These are the things I knew for sure about Miss Shaw from my own observance. She arrived at Shaw Jewelers before nine every morning, leaving plenty of time to polish the counters and arrange the pearls on the headless necks in the window before the store opened. She wore pumps that reminded me of the ones I'd seen once when Mama took me to the A&P Supermarket, the pretend princess shoes you could buy on the toy aisle, with plastic jewels across the toes and bottoms so stiff and curved that they arched your feet like a ballerina.

Every time I saw her, I wanted to stare, seeing how she held herself. To this day, I'll bet Miss Shaw practiced balancing books on her head while she walked around her house in those beautiful shoes.

And this one last important thing I knew about her. No one ever saw Miss Opal Shaw without her white Sunday gloves on, tiny buttons fastened against the soft underside of her wrists. She wore her gloves no matter if she was counting inky receipts or down-shifting her Cadillac convertible or presenting diamonds to a customer.

"I learned from that special penny how important the little things in life can be."

"I guess my sister and I got along the way most sisters do. I always felt like I was living in her shadow."

What *you* have to know is this: South St. Louis is not a place you'd want to wear white Sunday gloves on any other day of the week.

But I'd best get back to the penny.

I discovered Grace Kelly movies that summer, mostly because the Fox Theater had refrigerated air. The sign proclaimed in frozen-painted letters, AIR COOLED, with white x's to look like sparkles and icicles hanging from the A and the C. The Fox was so fancy that, after you paid at the box office, you got to pick any one of a dozen gleaming doors to walk through.

My big sister's temper matched the heat that July. Jean paced the house, as restless as the lynx that prowled its cage at the zoo, and about as moody, too. You could almost see the room get darker when she entered the door.

Jean, almost four years my senior, had graduated early. There wasn't a fourth grade one year, so the school board made it up by dividing the smart third graders from the ones who weren't so well off in that department. She acted like she'd won a Nobel Prize or something, when all she'd done was show up and go where they told her. Still, if I'd been in that class, they would have left me in the third grade, and Jean knew it. She bragged about moving up all the time. I guess I understood why. Sometimes, to survive Daddy's meanness, we got along best by acting big for our britches.

Jean's secretarial school would start in two months. Lately Mama had begun making offhanded suggestions about Jean taking me for an outing. "You go off to be a secretary soon, Jean, and you won't have time left to pal around with your sister," Mama would say as carefully as if she were tiptoeing on shattered glass. Even with that, Jean ignored me. She would slouch in the chair by the window and stare out the window with her arms crossed, a tragic yet slightly comic Jane Eyre.

I guess my sister and I got along the way most sisters do. I always felt like I was living in her shadow. She told me later how it bothered her I was always nipping at her heels. I told her she was wrong—I was just always trying to catch up with her.

We lived upstairs in a two-story flat on Wyoming Street, in a neighborhood where the buildings had been wedged much too close together. What had started as red brick, weathered and coated with coal soot, was now the color of brown rust. When the hot air rose, our rooms soaked up heat like an oven. The flat belonged to Daddy, and we could have lived downstairs if he'd wanted, but he reminded Mama every time she asked that he could get higher rent by keeping the paying tenants in the cooler rooms downstairs.

On the day of the penny, Jean had gone into another brood because Adele Middleton had invited her to spend the night with her family in an air-cooled room at the Ambassador Hotel but, as usual, Daddy had told her no. Daddy always said no to everything. Just because he was miserable, I don't know why he thought he had to spread that around to the rest of us, too.

Even when my sister was brooding, Jean was everything I wasn't: tall and willowy, with light brown hair and hazel eyes that flashed a hint of green. My hair looked like a fistful of cork grass when I wrestled it into a ponytail. Jean's hung straight down her back, as smooth as ribbon.

When she asked, "Why can't I go?" fear twisted in my throat the same way it did whenever Jean pushed it with Daddy. He would never change. And my sister seemed destined to be the one most willing to provoke his anger. I wanted to grab her and make her be quiet. But before I could, she blurted out, "Why not?"

My sister and I were many things to each other: sidekicks, rivals, accomplices, enemies. Some days we became an indecipherable muddle of all four. When I watched Jean stand up to Daddy, her bravery left me both aching with dread and reeling with love. I wanted to murder her for being so dim.

As Daddy ambled across the room toward her, his thick body moved with surprising agility. The anger in his pale green eyes looked like it could bore holes through my sister. A hank of his sparse brown hair, which he tried to keep combed across his balding scalp, fell forward onto his forehead. His thin, unpleasant lips curled.

"You talk back to me, girl, I'll knock you across the room."

"Jean." I picked up the goldfish bowl from the coffee table as he advanced on her. "Don't." I already knew it wouldn't help at all to go find Mama.

But Jean was too fiery for her own good. "You never let us do anything."

And just like that, Daddy grabbed her by the hair with a hand as broad as a fence board and landed a stinging smack across her face. She staggered over the coffee table, trying to shield herself with her left arm, but Daddy's punch to the stomach sent her sprawling to the floor. She landed hard on her rear. When she lifted her eyes to him, he said, "We don't got money for places like the Ambassador Hotel and you know it. You stop wanting what you can't pay for."

Jean stared up at Daddy in hatred. I knew what she must be thinking by the flash in her eyes. *Well, of course we've got money. You spend money all the time.*

It was an invitation, I wanted to cry to him, but I didn't dare. *When people invite you to do something, they don't intend for you to pay.*

The window fan did nothing but move the stifling air from one spot to another. Since the heat began, hardly any cars or people had been in sight, not even in Tower Grove Park. Sirens wailed out in the street. And Daddy kept right on going.

"I'll knock you down every time you glare at me like that. You hear me?"

It might have been the wrong thing to think, but I kept wondering if anything would come along that would knock *him* down.

"Come on." Jean clutched my hand so tight that the knobs of my knuckles crunched against each other. "Might not have enough for the Ambassador, but we do have enough for a picture show, Jenny." I knew she was using me to shield herself against Daddy, which made me feel a little important and terrified me all at the same time. I felt important because I was helping Jean. I was frightened because Daddy could just as well beat me up next. "*Rear Window* is on."

I tugged on Jean's arm and tried to make her look at me, but she wouldn't. If she met my eyes, one of us might have to admit that Daddy scared us. Nobody wanted to do that. It was safer to keep our minds filled with notions of Grace Kelly and Jimmy Stewart; we'd seen *Rear Window* twice already.

"*And you won't be able to take your eyes off her glowing beauty,*" the voiceover on the trailer touted with bated breath. I'd seen it so many times, I had the words memorized. "*She shares the heart and curiosity of James Stewart in this story of romance shadowed by the terror of a horrifying secret.*"

The delicate, sophisticated actress on safari

"I tugged on Jean's arm and tried to make her look at me, but she wouldn't. If she met my eyes, one of us might have to admit that Daddy scared us."

"The penny lay wheat-side up on the ground, so dirty as to almost be invisible."

with Clark Gable, the pioneer bride who protected Gary Cooper in a shootout, didn't seem all that remarkable to me. But the movies she played in, stories of girls-winning-out, pulled at my insides like the moon tugs at the Mississippi.

It was Jean who copied everything about Grace Kelly, from the hair she pulled into the shape of a dinner roll at the nape of her neck, to the dark glasses that made her look glamorous and mysterious at the same time, to the scarf she wore, as billowy as a spring cloud, knotted beneath her chin. Jean drove me crazy, the way she let thoughts of Grace Kelly dominate her life. Sometimes I thought I'd go nuts if she didn't stop talking about how Mr. Kelly's nickname for his daughter was Graciebird, or how her first commercial featured her spraying a can of insecticide around the room, or how, at the beginning, most directors she auditioned for found her too tall. I was sick to death of hearing the story of how, when Grace was a teenager, she stood on the front seat in a convertible and steered the car with her feet.

I was scrounging through my handbag, looking for my coin purse, thinking how my sister drove me out of my wits because she couldn't talk about anything besides Grace Kelly, when Jean came and dragged me down the narrow staircase. "Streetcar's coming," she said as I squinted against aching splinters of light. But she needn't have told me. The warning bell clanged as the door accordioned open and Jean shoved me up the steps. We lurched to the

rear to buy tickets and fell into warm, hard seats. My sister crossed her legs at the knees, shoved her sunglasses up over her forehead and drew out a tube of Pond's *Ever-So-Red* lipstick. She drew a neat circle around her mouth and blotted. When she snapped open her pocketbook to return the lipstick, I caught the beginning of what Jean's grown-up smell would be: a mixture of powder and faint-scented tissue and *Emeraude* cologne. The sweetness left my head aching and my stomach woozy.

When the trolley stopped in front of Woolworth's and we got off, Jean hurried across the street ahead of me to join the ticket line. Even from this distance, I could see the angry red handprint Daddy left on her cheek. She would be getting away from us soon. I couldn't breathe when I thought about Jean getting out of the house, going on to secretarial school.

"What are you staring at?" She plopped her hands on her hips. "Come on."

Often when we were by ourselves at home, when Daddy was gone, when Mama was outside and I was aching to share confidences with my sister, I'd catch Jean staring at me like she regretted knowing me. Maybe she didn't much like the idea that, due to the inopportune occurrence of my birth, she was tied to me for life. At times she almost seemed okay with having a sister. At other times, she made it plain she didn't like who her sister was. I couldn't do much to make it change, other than wish she'd try to see me differently. Jean's moods may have been a bother, I thought as I stood in the street outside the Fox Theater, but I wanted to stay on her good side. She was all I had.

That's when the streetcar clanged its bell and pulled away behind us.

That's the very moment I first saw the penny.

And that's the moment where this story really begins.

The penny lay wheat-side up on the ground, so dirty as to almost be invisible. Like I said, I wasn't accustomed to picking up pennies at that point. A penny is such a little thing—it's never been worth much. I stared at it, stepped over it, and headed toward my sister waiting outside the theater.

Then the noise of Grand Avenue went silent. *Go back*, something inside me insisted. *Don't miss the chance.*

To this day I have to wonder: What if I'd stepped over that penny and left it where it was? Or what if I'd knelt to the ground and grabbed the penny the first time around without stopping to think, if Jean hadn't turned toward me from the box office to holler, if she hadn't bossed me ("Okay, Jenny. Jenny, come on—*don't*. That's disgusting, picking things up in the street. You're washing your hands before you're getting anything from the snack bar."). Would everything have happened the same?

But I *did* walk past the penny at first. When something whispered, *Pick it up, Jenny—little things make a big difference*, my heart almost paused in my chest. And I knew it without a doubt. As surely as if someone well trusted had whispered it in my ear.

This moment has something to do with your destiny.

It was only a matter of seconds before I went back. Seconds, I found out later, that would change everything.

The copper had melted its way clear into the asphalt. I bent over—I still see it in my mind's eye—and used my fingernails to pry the hot coin out of the roadbed. I remember straightening up, the penny branding my palm right there in the middle of Grand Avenue. And that's when the mystifying chain of events began.

It started simple enough when the Pevely Dairy truck braked to keep from hitting me, which sent bottles, full and empty both, toppling sideways. A dozen or so dashed to the street and shattered with sharp cracks.

Glass flew. Daisies of milk splattered on the street. The door of the five-and-dime opened, and a woman lugging her baby in a car bed stepped outside just as the last three bottles fell. "Oh my word," the woman said, swinging the basket toward the building, shielding her child from what must have sounded like the Attack of the Killer Shards from Space. When she swung, she blindsided Bennett Mahaffey, who happened to be headed home with his favorite copy of Elvis Presley's "That's All Right (Mama)" tucked beneath his arm.

The blow struck Bennett hard enough to knock the LP from its jacket. When the disk hit the sidewalk, it wobbled on its edge and headed downhill toward everybody waiting in line at the Fox box office.

Bennett took off after his record. He wasn't running exactly, because you can't run after something that's doing the platter thing—rolling in a complete circle, then a smaller circle, until it starts to clatter to the ground. He loped after it with his arms widespread and his knees bent, making a tentative grab every time it came close, as if "That's All Right (Mama)" could actually go wheeling around like that and not get a scratch on it.

Now here's something about Miss Shaw that I didn't know—I didn't find it out until much later. Each Wednesday just after five in the evening, no matter whether it was snowing in

"To this day I have to wonder: What if I'd stepped over that penny and left it where it was? Or what if I'd knelt to the ground and grabbed the penny the first time around..."

St. Louis or blowing up a gale or hot as a skillet, Miss Shaw rearranged her display windows. Shaw Jewelers stood two doors to the north of the theater, its front door shaded by a green awning with silver letters, its scalloped edges lifting in the slight event of a breeze. Anyone who cared to watch could see her gloved hands working, removing a necklace here, a bracelet there, angling a set of earbobs, pushing a ring closer to the center.

Miss Shaw worked dutifully for some length of time, arranging gems, aligning chains, matching colors. Occasionally she would step out to gaze at the displays herself, tilting her head, assessing her artistry. Each time Miss Shaw stepped outside, she carried a polish rag in her pocket and necklaces draped across her gloves, often glancing to see if one of them would make the display more appealing.

On this particular day, Pete Mason happened to see Miss Shaw eyeing her windows from where he sat on a bench across the street. Indeed, he would say later, he had watched everything: the dairy truck, the swinging of the car bed, the crowd buying tickets for the picture show. He watched the stranger step off the curb, making a beeline for Miss Shaw. He watched the planned sleight of hand, the lifting of the necklaces from Miss Shaw's glove, and the bolting for cover into the box-office crowd.

"Hey!" Miss Shaw cried, too surprised for anything else.

That's how it happened that Pete Mason went into the crowd after the thief. That's how it happened that Bennett Mahaffey, who delivered appliances after school for Stix, Bauer, and Fuller, and who was the size of a small icebox himself, made a successful grab for his LP just as the fleeing looter, glancing back to gauge Pete's distance, tripped over Bennett instead. Bennett let out an "oomph" of breath that sounded like a tire going flat. The looter somersaulted to the ground. Miss Shaw raced toward the Fox Theater box office in her slender-heeled pumps. The man behind the window shouted, "Any more for *Rear Window*?"

"These yours?" Pete scooped up necklaces from where they'd flown to the sidewalk. He wiped them off with his monogrammed hanky.

"They are." Miss Shaw held out a gloved hand. "Thank you so much." It all happened in front of me, unfolding like a dream, where nothing's tied together but, in the end, the pieces make sense some way.

"Did you see that?" I ran to my sister's side, knowing she must have noticed something.

"What?"

"The truck." I pointed in the direction of the shattered bottles in the street. "Miss Shaw and her necklaces." I pointed in the opposite direction toward the green awning. I closed my fingers over the penny, which had cooled in my hand. *A moment to define my destiny.* That's when I saw Pete Mason nod his head toward me. Miss Shaw glanced in my direction and shot a warm, curious smile.

"Jenny Blake," Jean ordered, having missed the whole thing, "if you don't come on, we're going to miss the newsreels again." She sounded just as dour as always.

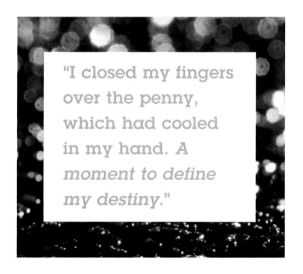

"I closed my fingers over the penny, which had cooled in my hand. *A moment to define my destiny.*"